To David & Piar,

I really like this man's writing! Probably because he's also a Ghosh.

Hope you like these books——

Sandra
03/01/2002

COUNTDOWN

Also by Amitav Ghosh

COUNTDOWN

Amitav Ghosh

RAVI DAYAL Publisher
Delhi

Published by
RAVI DAYAL Publisher
51 E Sujan Singh Park
New Delhi 110003

Distributed by
ORIENT LONGMAN LTD
Bangalore Bhubaneshwar Calcutta Chennai
Ernakulam Guwahati Hyderabad Jaipur
Lucknow Mumbai New Delhi Patna

First published 1999
Second impression 1999

ISBN 81 7530 025 6

Typeset by Rastrixi, New Delhi 110070
Printed at Rekha Printers Pvt. Ltd., New Delhi 110020

COUNTDOWN

The site where India's nuclear devices are tested lies close to a major national highway. This road runs most of the way through the state of Rajasthan, extending well into the Thar desert. The last stretch of the highway connects the old palace town of Bikaner to the fairy-tale desert fortress of Jaisalmer — a major tourist destination. The nuclear test site lies in between, some thirty miles from the district town of Pokharan. The town is small, but it boasts its own little medieval fortress.

On 11 May 1998, the Indian government tested five nuclear devices at the Pokharan site. I travelled there some three months later. My visit happened to coincide with the fifty-first anniversary of India's Independence, the start of the nation's second half-century as a free nation. As I was heading towards Pokharan, the Prime Minister, Mr Atal Bihari Vajpayee, was addressing the nation from the ramparts of Delhi's Red Fort — an Independence Day tradition. Speeding through the desert, I listened to him on the car radio.

Mr Atal Bihari Vajpayee's party, the Bharatiya Janata Party (B.J.P.), the largest single group in the coalition that now rules India, came to power in March 1998 and the Pokharan tests followed two months later. The tests occasioned great outpourings of joy on the part of the B.J.P.'s members and sympathizers. They organized festivities and handed out celebratory sweetmeats on the streets. There was talk of sending dust from the test site around the country so that the whole nation could partake in the glow of the blasts. Some of the B.J.P.'s leaders were said to be thinking of building a monument at Pokharan, a 'shrine of strength' that could be visited by pilgrims.

On 15 May, four days after the tests, the Prime Minister flew to Pokharan himself, accompanied by several members of his party. A celebration was organized on the crater left by the blasts. The Prime Minister was photographed standing on the crater's rim, throwing flowers into the pit. It was as though this were one of the crowning achievements of his life.

But three months later, speaking at the Red Fort, his voice sounded oddly subdued. The nuclear euphoria that followed the tests had faded quickly. On 28 May Pakistan had tested nuclear devices of its own, in response to the Pokharan tests. This had had a sobering effect. The rupee had fallen to a historic low, the stock market index had plummeted, prices had soared. The B.J.P.'s grasp on power was none too secure.

I was travelling to Pokharan with two men whom I'd met for the first time that morning. They were landowning farmers from the outskirts of Bikaner and they had relatives in Pokharan. A friend's friend had assigned them the task of showing me around. One of the men was in his sixties, with red, hennaed hair and a bushy moustache. The other was his son-in-law, a soft-spoken, burly man in his early forties. Their spoken Hindi had the distinctive lilt of western Rajasthan.

It was searingly hot, and the desert wind chafed like sandpaper against our eyes. Somewhere far ahead the shimmering line of the road seemed to melt into water. There were broods of peafowl in the thorny branches of the trees that lined the road. The birds took wing as the car shot past, their great tails iridescent in the sunlight trailing behind their bodies like painted sails. There was nothing but scrub to interrupt the eye's journey towards the horizon. In the dialect of the region, my guides told me, this area was known as 'the flat land'.

In Pokharan my guides were welcomed by their acquaintances. A town official said he knew exactly the man I ought to meet. This man was sent for and arrived half an hour later. His name was Manohar Joshi and he was thirty-six, bespectacled, with a ready smile. He'd grown up in Pokharan, he told me. He was twelve in 1974, when a nuclear device was first tested in the district. The then Prime Minister was Indira Gandhi.

'In the years after 1974' said Manohar Joshi, 'there was so much illness here that people didn't have money to buy pills. We had never heard of cancer before in this area. But people began to get cancer after the test. There were strange skin diseases. People used to scratch themselves all the time. There were sores on their skin. If these things had happened anywhere else in the country, in Bihar or Kashmir, people would rise up and stop it. But people here don't protest, they are too quiescent; they'll put up with anything.'

Growing up in Pokharan, Manohar Joshi had developed a strong interest in nuclear matters. He had read everything he could find on the subject. His family hadn't had the resources to send him to college. After high school he'd started to work in a shop. But all the while he'd wanted to write. He'd begun to send opinion pieces to Hindi newspapers. Eventually one of them had taken him on as a stringer.

On the afternoon of 11 May, he was preparing for his siesta when the ground began to shake, almost throwing him off his cot. He knew at once that this was no earthquake: this was a more powerful jolt than that of 1974. He recognized it for what it was and called his paper immediately. This made him, Mr Joshi said proudly, the first journalist in the world to learn of the tests.

Mr Joshi told me about a village called Khetoloi: it was just six kilometres from the test site, the nearest human habitation. The effects of the tests of 1974 had been felt more severely here than anywhere else in the district. The same was true of the most recent tests.

We headed into the scrub, along a dirt road. The village was small but evidently well-off. There were no huts or shanties here: the houses were sturdily built, of stone and mortar.

Khetoloi was an unusual village, Mr Joshi explained. Its inhabitants made their living mainly from the tending of livestock and had grown prosperous at this trade. Almost everyone in the village was literate, women as well as men. They were Bishnois, members of a small religious sect whose founder had forbidden the felling of trees and killing of animals. They thought of themselves as the world's first conservationists.

We stopped to look at a couple of houses whose walls had been split by the tests of 11 May. Within minutes we were surrounded by eager schoolchildren. They led us into a house where three turbaned elders were sitting on charpais, talking.

On 11 May, they told me, at about noon a squad of soldiers had driven up and asked the villagers to move out of their houses to open ground. They guessed what was going to happen. Some of them possessed refrigerators and television sets. They carried these out of doors and set them down in the sand, under the noonday sun. Then they sat under trees and waited. It was very hot. The temperature touched 48 degrees centigrade.

At about two thirty there was a tremendous shaking

in the ground and a booming noise. They saw a great cloud of dust and black and white smoke shooting skywards in the distance. Cracks opened up in the walls of some of their houses. Some of them had built underground tanks to store water for their livestock. The blasts split the tanks, emptying them of water.

Later an official came around and offered them small sums of money as compensation. The underground tanks were very expensive. The villagers refused to accept the money they were offered and demanded more.

Political activists came to the village and erected a colourful awning. There was talk that the B.J.P. would hold celebrations in Khetoloi. By this time the villagers were enraged, and they let everyone know. The tent was moved away, for fear that the media would get wind of the villagers' complaints.

'The only people who benefit from these tests are the politicians', said a young man. 'They bring no benefits to anyone else in the country.'

This young man was very articulate and the elders had handed him the burden of the conversation. He was a villager himself, he said, but he held a clerical job and his salary was paid by the government. He wouldn't give me his name and nor did I press him.

'After the test', said the clerk, 'the Prime Minister said he'd been to Pokharan and nothing had happened, there was no radioactivity. But how long was he here? Radioactivity doesn't work in minutes.'

Before the tests of 1974, he said, cancer was unknown to Khetoloi. Since that time some ten to fifteen people had died of the disease. Many had suffered from inexplicable skin rashes.

'It always starts up when it rains', he said. 'Sores and boils appear on the skin. Even cows and camels get sores on their hide. It's as though the grass itself is covered with radioactivity.'

Since 1974, he said, some twenty children had been born with deformities in the limbs. Cows had developed tumours in their udders. Calves were born blind, and with their tongues and eyes attached to the wrong parts of their faces. No one had heard of such things before.

In the past, said the clerk, the villagers had always tried to co-operate with the government. They hadn't publicized their complaints and they'd been careful when talking to the press. 'But now we are fed up. What benefits do we get from these tests? We don't even have a hospital here — all we've got is a health centre with one nurse.'

Someone brought a tray of water glasses. The clerk saw me hesitate and began to laugh. 'Outsiders never want to drink our water', he said. 'Even the people who come to tell us that everything is safe won't touch our water.'

My guides were subdued on the drive back to Bikaner. Even though they lived in the neighbouring district, it was years since they'd last been to Pokharan. What we'd seen had come as a complete surprise.

That evening I walked around the royal palace of Bikaner — a part of it is now a hotel. The palace was vast, empty and beautiful, in the way of a melancholy fantasy. The pink stone of which it was built seemed to turn translucent in the light of the setting sun. The construction was of a stupefying lavishness. An emerald swimming pool glowed on the floor of a high-ceilinged room, surrounded by soaring marble pillars. The wall on one side was of pink stone latticework; on the other, doors with stained-glass panels opened into a garden and a dusty tennis court.

The palace was built at the turn of the century by Maharaja Sir Ganga Singh of Bikaner — a luminary who had cut a very splendid figure in the British Raj. He had entertained Viceroys and sent troops to Flanders during the First World War. He was one of the signatories of the Treaty of Versailles. There were pictures in the corridors of the palace depicting great moments of Maharaja Ganga Singh's life; he is shown in the company of such figures as Winston Churchill, Lloyd George and so on.

In New Delhi many people had talked to me about how nuclear weapons would help India achieve 'great power status'. I'd been surprised by the depth of emotion that was invested in that curiously archaic phrase 'great power'. What would it mean, I'd asked myself, to the lives of working journalists, salaried technocrats and so on if India achieved 'great power status'? What were the images that were evoked by this tag?

Now, walking through this echoing old palace, looking at the pictures in the corridors, this aspiration took on, for the first time, the contours of an imagined reality. This was what the nuclearists wanted: to sign treaties, to be pictured with the world's powerful, to hang portraits on their walls, to become ancestors. On the bomb they had pinned their hopes of bringing it all back.

The man who is regarded as the strategic mastermind behind India's nuclear policies is K. Subrahmanyam, a civilian defence affairs expert. He is sixty-five, a large, forceful man who was until recently the Director of the Indian Institute of Strategic Studies.

Subrahmanyam's advocacy of an aggressive nuclear programme is premised on the view that nuclear weapons are the currency of global power. 'Nuclear weapons are not military weapons', he told me. 'Their logic is that of international politics. The international system of security has been progressively brought under a global nuclear order that provides for the hegemony of the five nuclear weapons powers. India wants to be a player and not an object of this global nuclear order.'

I had expected to hear a great deal about regional threats and the Chinese missile programme. But as Subrahmanyam sees it, India's nuclear policies are only tangentially related to the question of India's military security. They are aimed at something much more distant and very much more grand: the global distribution of power. In Subrahmanyam's view, India could, if it plays its cards right, parlay its nuclear programme into a seat at the United Nations' Security Council, and earn universal recognition as a 'global player'.

Subrahmanyam told me a story: it was about a Hollywood film he'd seen many years ago. It was called *A Million Pound Note*, and it featured Gregory Peck. In the film the character played by Peck shows that even as valueless a piece of paper as a million pound note can be used to con tradesmen into extending credit.

'A nuclear weapon acts like a million pound note', Subrahmanyam said, his eyes gleaming with mischievous glee. 'It is apparently of no use. You can't use it to stop small wars. But it buys you credit and that gives you the power to intimidate.'

India's nuclear programme in other words has nothing to do with defending the country: it is a kind of ploy, a minting of false coin in the hope of purchasing worldwide influence.

Subrahmanyam bristled when I suggested that there might be certain inherent dangers to the possession of nuclear weapons. Like most Indian hawks, he considers himself a reluctant nuclearist. He would prefer to see nuclear weapons done away with altogether, he says. It is the nuclear superpowers' insistence on maintaining their arsenals that makes this an impossible dream.

Issues of safety, he told me, were no more pressing in India than anywhere else. India and Pakistan had lived with each others' nuclear programmes for many years; their experience in this regard had been much smoother than that of other countries. 'It was the strategic logic of the west that was madness. Think of the United States building 70,000 nuclear weapons at a cost of $3.5 trillion. Do you think these people have any claim to rationality? Are they in a position to preach to anybody? They should learn from us. We have nothing to learn from them.'

Subrahmanyam, like many other Indians who support the nuclear programme, sees very little danger in the deployment of nuclear weapons. For many the bomb is not a weapon at all, but merely a counter in the game of global power politics. In New Delhi it is widely believed that the very immensity of the destructive potential of nuclear weapons renders them useless as instruments of war, ensuring that their deployment can never be anything other than symbolic. The fact that the United States and Russia were able to manage their gargantuan arsenals without going to war is taken to be proof of this: Indian experts see no reason why

India or Pakistan should be thought any less capable of managing a nuclear stand-off than were the United States and the Soviet Union.

The idea that nuclear war is unthinkable — the premise on which the Cold War was managed — has thus led to a paradoxical result. It has given nuclear weapons an aura of harmlessness, freeing them, as it were, to be thought of purely as symbols. Those who believe that India should acquire nuclear weapons see the bomb principally as an icon of empowerment.

'The bomb is a champagne bottle', one journalist said to me. 'It'll lie in a corner gathering dust. There will be no first strikes and nor will there be any planning for one. Our bomb is at best a minimum deterrent. No one would ever contemplate using it.'

I went to see an old acquaintance, Chandan Mitra, a historian with an Oxford doctorate. I had come across an article of his entitled 'Explosion of Self-Esteem', published shortly after the tests of 11 May. In Delhi University, when I first knew Chandan, he was a Marxist.

'The bomb is the global currency of self-esteem' Chandan told me, with disarming bluntness. 'And what two hundred years of colonialism did to us was that it robbed us of our self-esteem. We do not have any degree of national pride or national cohesion in the same way as the British have, the French have, the Germans have, the Americans have. We have been told systematically that we are really not fit to rule ourselves — that was the whole justification of colonialism. Our achievements, our worth, our talent was always negated and denied. Mahatma Gandhi's endeavour throughout the freedom movement was to rebuild our sense of self-esteem. Even if you don't have guns, he said, you still have moral force. Now fifty years down the line we know that moral force isn't enough to survive in this world: it doesn't count for very much. When you look at India today and ask how best you can instil a sense of national pride or overcome those feelings of inferiority which have been ingrained in your mind for two hundred years, the bomb seems to be as good an answer as any.'

'What about you and me Chandan?' I asked. 'Do you think we carry this sense of inferiority within us?'

'We're as good as anyone else', he said. 'But we have this problem of being treated as inferiors, or being patronized. When we have to prove ourselves internationally, we have to shout louder than anyone else.'

Chandan is not the only Indian who regards the tests as a primal scream of self-assertion. Everywhere in the country I met people who thought that the tests would lead to more respectful and deferential treatment for India and Indians. I have in front of me a letter written to the magazine *Science*, by Dr G. Padmanabhan, the Director of the Indian Institute of Science in Bangalore. 'The recent nuclear test explosions have created a tremendous euphoria in

India', he writes. 'India has many, many problems, but we are tired of being depicted in the West as having negative qualities. Given this treatment, one clutches at any "victory" that makes one feel like an entity to be counted.'

For Chandan as for many other Indians, the bomb is much more than a weapon and it concerns matters much larger than a mere defence policy. It is a great vessel filled with all the unfulfilled aspirations and thwarted dreams of the last fifty years — ambitions of a larger and grander place in the world, for a re-arrangement of global power, for a rebirth of national pride. With the tests of 11 May these nebulous hopes and dreams found the symbol they had been looking for. The bomb became the banner of a political insurgency, a kind of millenarian movement.

The landscape of India teems with such insurgencies: the country is seized, in V.S. Naipaul's eloquent phrase, with 'a million mutinies now'. These insurrections are perhaps the most remarkable product of Indian democracy, this enabling of once-marginal groups to fight for places at the table of power. The bomb-cult represents the uprising of those who find themselves being pushed back from this table: it is the rebellion of the rebelled-against, the insurrection of an élite.

The leaders of the bomb-cult see themselves as articulating the aspirations of an immeasurably vast constituency: the figures most often cited are of a magnitude of nine hundred million people — 'one sixth of humanity', in the words of the Indian Prime Minister. The reality however is that the number of its followers is very much smaller than this and is dwindling every day: the almost-mystical rapture that greeted the unveiling of the cult's fetish has long since dissipated.

In August 1998 I went to the Lok Sabha, to watch a debate on the foreign policy fallout of the recent tests. In India, as in most democracies, on matters of national security and foreign policy, politicians have usually come together no matter what their other differences. On 4 August it was clear that this consensus had been destroyed forever: of the members who spoke the majority were vociferously critical of the Government for permitting the tests. Several of the speeches were ringing denunciations of the Bharatiya Janata Party's nuclear policies.

Some of the most eloquent of these speeches came from the leaders of traditionally disadvantaged groups. I later went to see one of the leaders who spoke that day, Mr Ram Vilas Paswan. Mr Paswan is a Dalit — a member of a caste group that was once treated as untouchable by high-caste Hindus. Mr Paswan holds the distinction of winning his parliamentary seat by the record margin of four hundred thousand votes. He was the Railway Minister in the short-lived government that preceded Vajpayee's and is today something of a cult hero among many of the country's three hundred million Dalits.

Mr Paswan is a wiry man with a close-cropped beard and gold-rimmed eyeglasses. 'These nuclear tests were not in the Indian national interest', he told me.

'They were done in the interests of a party, to keep the present government from imploding from within. In the last elections the present Prime Minister of Pakistan, Mr Nawaz Sharif, campaigned on a platform of better relations with India. For this he was pilloried by his opponent Benazir Bhutto but he still won with a massive mandate. This means that the people of Pakistan want friendship with India. But how did our government respond? It burst a bomb in the face of a man who had reached out to us in friendship. And this in a country where ordinary citizens don't have food to eat. Where villages are being washed away by floods. Where prices are touching the skies. Of the country's six hundred thousand villages, one-third don't have arrangements for safe drinking water. Fifty per cent of our people live below the poverty line. For the price of a single battle tank we could open one hundred primary schools. But what we do instead is that every year we spend thirty-five thousand crores of rupees on armaments.'

On 6 August, Hiroshima Day, I was in Calcutta. More than one hundred thousand people marched in the streets in protest against the nuclear tests of 11 May. It was plain that the cult of the bomb had few adherents here; that the tests had divided the country more deeply than ever.

India's first atomic test was conducted in Pokharan, in 1974. I was eighteen at the time, in my second year in college, at Delhi University. The tests were ordered by Indira Gandhi the then Prime Minister.

I remember being astonished at the great rush of popularity that followed on this imagery of annihilation; the enormous groundswell of public support. The voices of dissent were few: all the major political parties, right- and left-wing alike, came out in support of the test.

George Fernandes, the present Defence Minister, was one of the very few political figures who sounded a note of criticism. This took real courage at that time, a genuine spirit of independence. For those such as myself, people who were opposed to nuclear energy in an instinctive, perhaps un-reflective, way Fernandes became a kind of beacon. I began to think of him as one of the few polit-ical figures in the country of whom I could say, without shame, that he spoke for me and my opinions.

Eight months later Indira Gandhi dissolved Par-liament, froze all political and legislative processes and suspended civil rights: thus began the period that was known as the Emergency. Several politicians

were arrested. Fernandes went into hiding, prompt-
ing a nationwide manhunt.

The Emergency was still in place in 1976 when I
emerged from college with a B.A. degree. I succeeded
in getting a job as a trainee journalist at the *Indian
Express*, which was then one of the few papers in the
country that was openly critical of the regime. This
was my first job and I loved it.

The *Express* newsroom was as unadorned as the
inside of a shoe-box. It was riotously noisy, with bare
concrete walls that caught and amplified every sound.
The printing plant was immediately below, so we
were constantly on our knees, stuffing wads of paper
under vibrating chairs and tables. The room stretched
the length of a large building and troops of food-ven-
dors, tea-boys and paan-wallahs circulated through it
all day, shuttling from the far end, where the sub-
editors sat, to the other, where the city-desk reporters
lounged around a bank of gap-toothed typewriters,
their feet propped up beside their motorcycle helmets.
We thrived on the camaraderie of defiance, sustaining
ourselves on the rumours and political gossip that
went flying around the newsroom. George Fernandes
was the hero of many of these stories.

Eventually Indira Gandhi capitulated and fresh
elections were called. I was on duty at the *Express*
sub-editing desk the day the results started coming
in. Our editors had erected a huge board outside the
building. People began to gather in ones and twos in
the late afternoon. By evening there were thousands

of people outside. Every update was greeted with cheers. Indira Gandhi and her party were routed; she lost her seat by a margin of twenty thousand votes. Fernandes contested the election from the cell where he had been imprisoned by Mrs Gandhi. He won by a huge margin.

A new government was formed by a coalition of parties. Fernandes was now a star; one of the architects of this democratic revolution. He became Minister of Commerce.

This was a moment of euphoric hope in India: many believed that a stable party system would evolve, that no one group or personality would ever again dominate the nation's politics as the Congress and the Nehru-Gandhi family had in the past.

But then came an astonishing turnabout: it was Fernandes who destroyed the new government. Sixteen months after the election, without any proper accounting or explanation, he resigned his ministership and withdrew from the cabinet. The coalition was too shaky to survive his departure. It collapsed. Once again, fresh elections, and a few months later Mrs Indira Gandhi was back in power.

It was now Fernandes' turn to lose his parliamentary seat. Unlike most Indian politicians he has never had a vote bank that he could call his own — no caste group or regional constituency that could be counted on in moments of difficulty. A long time went by before he won another election: for years he was just another journeyman in the political wilderness.

There was a brief period during Fernandes' lean years when I saw a good deal of him. This was in November 1984, in the weeks following Mrs Indira Gandhi's assassination by her Sikh bodyguards. There were terrible riots in New Delhi and thousands of Sikhs were killed. In response to this violence citizens' groups mushroomed all over the city. Some attempted to provide supplies and medical care for the victims; some began to investigate the killings. Fernandes took an active part in these efforts. No one who watched him could doubt that he was appalled by this horrific spectacle of sectarian violence.

In New Delhi in the aftermath of the tests I went to see George Fernandes, at the Defence Ministry in 'South Block'.

South Block is the nerve centre of India's networks of power. New Delhi is a vast, sprawling city of some nine million people, but its government offices and institutions are concentrated in a very small area. This part of the capital was designed and built by the prominent British architect, Sir Edwin Lutyens, in the waning years of the British Raj. Two gargantuan buildings form the bureaucratic core of the city. They are known simply as North Block and South Block and they face each other across a broad boulevard. The buildings are of red sandstone and they are ornamented with many turrets and gateways of Anglo-Oriental design. But the embellishments cannot disguise the fact that these structures are fundamentally nothing other than blocks — vast rectangular edifices that lie upon a hill like two gigantic catafalques.

From this fantastically grandiose complex the power of the Indian state radiates outwards in diminishing circles of effectiveness. It is here that the Prime Minister, the Foreign Minister, the Defence Minister and the Home Minister have their offices; it is here that the country's most powerful ministries are housed.

I was taken to Fernandes' office in the Defence Ministry by Jaya Jaitley, the secretary of the political party to which he belongs. I had never imagined that I would one day be striding into the Defence Ministry. Yet the idea that I was there now was certainly no more unlikely than the thought that these offices were presided over by George Fernandes, that perennially indignant activist. That this was possible at all was clear evidence of some great churning in the body politic, some sort of crisis.

As a teenager Fernandes had harboured ambitions of becoming a Catholic priest. At the age of sixteen he rebelled against his father and joined a lay order seminary. He spent three years in seminaries, growing steadily more disillusioned as he grew older: he remembers being appalled that the Rectors ate better food than the seminarian and sat at higher tables. It seemed intolerable to him that such divisions should exist among those who were trying to create a community centred around *alteri Christi*, the body of Christ. At the age of nineteen he left the seminary and soon afterwards became a convinced socialist. He went to Bombay and joined the trade union movement. For many years he had no settled home, no permanent address. He would live with members of his union, a few nights at a time, on the outskirts of various Bombay factories. His father disowned him and he did not visit his home again until he was in his forties.

Fernandes still considers himself a socialist. The party he belongs to now is a small splinter group called the Samata Party. In the elections held in February 1998, the Samata Party succeeded in winning two seats out of a total of five hundred and fifty. The overall results of the elections were only marginally different from the one before. It gave the B.J.P., with a hundred and fifty seats, a slight edge over the Congress which had one hundred and forty. The B.J.P. is openly hostile to the secularism that is enshrined in India's constitution. Its programmes and ideology are based on an assertive and militant vision of Hinduism. In 1992 members of the B.J.P. were instrumental in organizing the demolition of the Babari Masjid that stood upon a site they believed to be sacred to Hindus. In the aftermath of this there were riots across the Indian subcontinent and many thousands of people died.

After the elections it was evident that small parties would tip the balance. The Samata Party entered the ruling coalition on very advantageous terms, securing two positions in the cabinet, Fernandes' included. Fernandes has been one of the most visible figures in the cabinet ever since the new government was formed.

We went up to Fernandes' office in the Minister's elevator. A soldier in sparkling white puttees and a red turban pressed the buttons. The doors of Fernandes' office were open. We walked in and found him at his desk.

Fernandes is sixty-eight but could pass for a man in his mid-forties. He is lean, square-jawed, with a full head of curly greying hair. He dresses always in long homespun cotton kurtas and loose pajamas. On his feet he wears leather sandals. He never wears socks or shoes if he can help it and he never allows his clothes to be ironed. For Fernandes these garments are a statement of simplicity, adopted in his early days as a trade unionist and never abandoned.

A couple of senior officers marched in. I watched Fernandes as he turned away to talk to them: it was clear at a glance that despite his slippers and unironed clothes he was not at all put out by the officers' heel-clicking starchiness; indeed there seemed to be a genuine warmth between them. It occurred to me that Fernandes too was in a kind of uniform; that there was something about the studied deliberateness of his costume that spoke of a not-inconsiderable personal vanity, an absorbing concern with appearances.

The room was large but dank. Two pictures hung high on the walls, dominating the room. One was a portrait of Mahatma Gandhi; the other was a picture of the ruins of Hiroshima, of the blasted remains of a church. It struck me that it was probably right here, at this desk, under these pictures that Fernandes had signed off on the tests of 11 May.

It was lunchtime now: we decided to go out. Fernandes led the way to a staircase that spiralled down one of Lutyens' turret-like stairwells. Just as we were starting down the stairs I spotted a small, simian figure observing us from a dimly-lit landing. I stopped, startled. It was a monkey, a common rhesus, with a muddy brown mantle and a bright red belly. The animal stared at me calmly, unalarmed, and then went bounding off into the corridors of the Defence Ministry.

'Did you see that monkey?' I said foolishly.

Fernandes laughed. 'Yes. There's a whole troop living on this staircase.' 'Sometimes', one of his aides added in an undertone, 'they attack the generals . . . '

At lunch I said to Fernandes: 'Are you really completely comfortable with the recent nuclear tests? I ask you this because I have read your anti-nuclear writings and seen you at peace marches.'

Fernandes said: 'I have been opposed to the bomb from day one till the 19th of July 1996. On that day the Lok Sabha was debating the Comprehensive Test Ban Treaty and we had various meetings on this. In these discussions there was one point of unanimity.

All the parties agreed that we would not sign this treaty. I went through deep anguish — an atom bomb was morally unacceptable to me. I had campaigned against, spoken against it in various universities and other fora. But I said that if today the five nations which have nuclear weapons tell us how to behave and what weapons we should have, then we should keep all our options open — every option. I did not say that we should make the bomb. But that was implied.'

His mood turned sombre as we talked. 'I don't think many Indians care about the country', he said. 'By Indians I mean those in the highest places. If they cared they wouldn't have been looting the treasuries as they are and they wouldn't be allowing the crooks of the world to treat this country as a grazing ground. Some day we will sink and this is not anything to do with China or with Pakistan. It is because this country is cursed to put up with a leadership that has chosen to sell it for their own personal aggrandizement.'

I was struck by the note of despair in his voice. It was hard to believe that this was the country's Defence Minister speaking, a politician who had reached the pinnacle of his career.

My conversation with Chandan had ended on a similar note. I found the very fact of this even more unsettling than what Fernandes had said. Chandan is young and extremely successful, a man who ought to be basking in the afterglow of seeing the B.J.P.

in its first season in power. But just before we parted he said: 'This is the worst it's ever been in India. We have hit rock bottom.'

Evidently the cult of the bomb, like all millenarian movements, was as much a product of despair as of hope. How had this come about? As a nation India has more or less played by the rules of democracy, keeping to a middle path in most things. How had matters come to such a pass that reasonable people could argue that the country needed to risk annihilation in order to repair the damage sustained by its self-esteem?

After lunch, as he was rising to leave Fernandes told me that he was scheduled soon to visit certain military installations in the embattled state of Kashmir. From there he planned to fly further north, to Ladakh, and the Siachen glacier in the Karakoram mountains. Across these snows, at altitudes of up to twenty-one thousand feet, Indian and Pakistani troops have been exchanging fire every day for fifteen years.

Fernandes was taking a party of journalists with him, in his plane. The trip was to be a tour of inspection but he would also address some political meetings. If I wanted to join him, he said, I should let his office know.

I know very few politicians, and none certainly who have lived as close to the centre of post-Independent India's history as has George Fernandes. Perhaps he would have some answers.

On the morning of 24 August I boarded an Indian Air Force plane with Fernandes and his entourage. The plane was a twin-engined AN-32, an elderly and unabashedly functional craft of Soviet manufacture.

We had lunch at a large military base in eastern Kashmir. Fernandes met with a warmly enthusiastic reception: it was clear that he was very popular, among soldiers and officers alike.

At lunch I found myself sharing a table with several major-generals and other senior officers. Some of their names were familiar to me: they were from old soldiering families and I had read about their relatives in books of history. Their fathers and grandfathers had fought for the British Empire in Flanders, North Africa, Italy and Burma. But their sons and daughters, I was interested to learn, had for the most part broken with these family traditions, choosing to become computer engineers, bankers, lawyers and the like. Evidently, even among those for whom being a general was a family business, soldiering in the Indian Army no longer held its old appeal.

I was interested to learn of these senior officers' view of the nuclear tests, but I soon discovered that their curiosity on this score far exceeded mine. Did I know who was behind the decision to proceed with the tests? they asked. Who had issued the orders? Who exactly had known in advance?

I could no more enlighten them than they could me: only in India, I thought to myself, could a writer and a tableful of generals ask each other questions like these. It was confirmation, at any rate, that the armed forces' role in the tests had been minimal at best.

I soon learnt also that the views of military personnel were by no means uniform. Many believe very strongly that India needs a nuclear deterrent; some feel that the tests of 11 May have resulted in certain security benefits for both India and Pakistan by bringing their secret nuclear programmes into the open: that the two countries would now exercise greater caution in their frequent border confrontations.

But some others expressed private apprehensions. 'An escalation of hostilities along the border can happen very easily', a major-general said to me. 'It takes just one officer in the field to start off a series of escalations. There's no telling where it will stop.'

None of the generals, I was relieved to note, appeared to believe that nuclear weapons were harmless icons of empowerment: in the light of some of my earlier conversations around the country, there was something almost reassuring in this.

After lunch we went by helicopter to Surankote, an army base located on the neck of territory that connects Kashmir to India. Fernandes was to inspect the base and address a gathering.

The base was set in a valley, between steep, verdant hills. The sunlight glowed golden and mellow on the surrounding slopes as we landed. The base was fenced off, and the perimeters of the garrison were manned by guards with machine-guns ready at their waists.

We were whisked off the landing pad and taken quickly into the interior of the base. I found myself riding in a vehicle with a young major.

'What's it like here?' I said.

'Bad.' He laughed. 'Bordering on terrible.' He had the coiled alertness of someone whose nerves have been wound to the extreme edge of tautness.

The Pakistani front lines were just a few miles away, he explained. It took just a day to walk over the hills. This camp lay astride the main route used by those who wanted to cross from one side to the other. Nowhere in the state was the tension so great as it was here.

Fernandes had mounted a podium with several other politicians and local dignitaries. A crowd of a few hundred people had gathered to hear them. Behind them were green hills, capped by clouds.

The major pointed at the hills. 'While we're standing here talking there are half a dozen operations going on in those hills, right there.'

He led me aside. 'Let the politicians talk', he said. 'I'll show you what's happening here if you want to know.'

We went into a tent and the major seated himself at a radio set. 'This is where we listen to them', he said. He scanned the wavelengths, tuning into several exchanges.

'Listen', he said, turning up the volume. 'They're

speaking Punjabi, not Kashmiri. They're mercenaries who've signed up on two-year contracts. They're right there, in those hills.'

The voices on the radio had a slow, dreamlike quality; they were speaking to each other unhurriedly, calling out cheerful greetings in slow-cadenced rural Punjabi. I had no idea who the voices belonged to.

As we were leaving the tent, the major darted suddenly into a group of people and took some rolls of film from a photographer. 'I can't trust them', he said. 'I don't know what they've taken pictures of. I can't trust anyone here.'

We walked back to the crowd to listen to the speeches. 'The politicians talk so well', the major said, his eyes flickering over the crowd. 'But what we have here is a war. Does anyone know what's happening here? Does anyone care?'

The crowd was quiet and orderly; the people in it looked as though they had dressed up for the afternoon. After Fernandes had spoken, he was besieged by petitioners, asking for jobs, roads, schools.

Fernandes is very well acquainted with the situation in Kashmir: he knows it better than almost any other Indian politician. During one of his terms as a minister he functioned as a special reporter on Kashmir. He talks often of those days and of how he drove into the Kashmir countryside, all but alone, meeting insurgents informally, militants and local leaders, listening to people's grievances, to their

stories of brutalization at the hands of the police
and the army. Not the least of the many ironies of
Fernandes' present position is that he was once the
country's most prominent campaigner against
human rights violations by the army. He is on record
as having once described an Indian Army operation
as 'a naked dance of a bunch of sadists and criminals
in uniform'.

As I watched the petitioners clamouring around
Fernandes, I began to wonder what it would be like
to try to live an everyday life, the life of schools
and jobs, in a village that was sandwiched between
that base, with its bristling perimeter fence, and the
mountains beyond with their hidden guns and dis-
embodied voices. A line quoted by the Kashmiri
poet, Agha Shahid Ali kept coming to mind: *'They
make a desolation and call it peace.'* But here peace
was not even a pretence.

Next day we flew to Leh, the principal town in
India's northernmost district, Ladakh. As the
crow flies, Ladakh is only a few hundred miles from
the valley of Kashmir, but it is a world apart, a niche
civilization, as it were — a far outpost of Tibetan
Buddhist culture that has flourished in a setting even
more extreme, in climate, altitude and topography,
than that of Tibet.

Leh's altitude is twelve thousand feet. On landing,

we were handed pills to prevent altitude sickness and warned of short-term memory loss. In the afternoon, driving towards the Siachen glacier, we went spiralling over the 18,300 foot Khardung Pass. A painted sign announced this to be the world's highest motorable road. Ahead lay the Karakoram mountains: among the peaks in this range is the 28,000 foot K2, Mount Godwin-Austen, the second highest mountain in the world.

The landscape was of a lunar desolation, with electric-blue skies and a blinding sun. Great sheets of glaciated rock rose sheer out of narrow valleys: their colours were the unearthly pinks and mauves of planetary rings and stellar moons. The mountains rose to sharp, pyramidal points, their ridges honed to fine, knife-like edges. Their slopes were covered with pulverized rock, as though they had been rained upon by torrents of gravel. Along the valley floors, beside ribbon-like streams, there were trees with whispering leaves and silver bark. On an occasional sandbank, dwarfed by the vastness of the landscape, there were tidy little monasteries and villages, sur-rounded by fantailed green terraces.

Outside the polar snows there is perhaps no terrain on earth that is less hospitable, less tolerant of human claims, than the region around the Karakorams. There are no demarcated borders here. In Kashmir there is a Line of Control that serves as a de facto border. This agreed-upon line stops short of this region, ending at an observation post named NJ 9842.

The Line of Control was a product of the first war between India and Pakistan. In 1948 both countries signed an agreement on this line. At the time neither India nor Pakistan thought of extending this line into the high Karakorams. 'No one had ever imagined,' a Pakistani academic said to me, in Lahore, 'that human beings would ever wish to claim these frozen places.'

But it was the very challenge of the terrain that led to the making of these claims. In the late 1970s and early '80s several international mountaineering expeditions ventured into this region. They came through Pakistan and used Pakistani-controlled areas as their roadheads. This raised suspicions in India. It was discovered that maps were being published in the United States with lines drawn through the region, suggesting delineated borders where none existed. There was talk of 'cartographic aggression'.

It was these notional lines, on maps used mainly by mountaineers, that were eventually to transform the Siachen glacier into a battleground. It is generally agreed that the glacier has absolutely no strategic, military or economic value whatsoever. It is merely an immense, slowly moving mass of compacted snow and ice, seventy miles long and over a mile deep.

In 1983, in order to stake India's territorial claims, the Indian army launched a massive airlifting operation and set up a number of military posts along the glacier. Pakistan responded by putting up a parallel line of posts. There was no agreement on which posts should be where: shoving was the only way to decide.

Since that time, every day, for fifteen years, the Indian and Pakistani armies have been exchanging barrages of artillery fire at heights that range from ten to twenty thousand feet.

We stopped to visit a dimly-lit hospital ward. There were some dozen men inside. None of them had been injured by 'enemy action': it was the terrain that was their principal adversary. They were plains-men mainly: in the normal course of things snow would play no part at all in their lives. They were not volunteers: only officers volunteer for service on the glacier. Some of the men were in their twenties, but most were older, some possibly in their late-thirties and perhaps even early forties — family men, whose bodies had no doubt begun to slow down a little even before they were sent here. They stared at us mutely and we stared back, trying to think of something cheerful to say. One of them had tears in his eyes.

At some posts on the glacier, temperatures dip sometimes to −40 and −50 degrees centigrade. At these altitudes wind velocities are very high. The soldiers live in tents that are pitched either on the surface of the glacier or on ledges of rock. Shooting at the other side takes up very little of their time. They spend much of their time crammed inside their tents. Such heat as they have comes from small kerosene stoves. These are kept going all night and all day. Kerosene produces a foul-smelling grimy kind of soot. This soot works itself slowly into the soldiers' clothes, their hair, their eyes, their nostrils. When they walk back to their base camps, after their three-month tours of duty, they are enveloped in black grime.

The posts on the glacier are supplied mainly by helicopter. The craft used for this purpose is the Cheetah, a lightweight helicopter, descended from a French prototype, the Alouette. The Cheetah has been in production in India for some thirty years. On the glacier it is frequently required to perform beyond its capabilities. The Cheetah requires a two-man pilot team which means that on some sorties the craft can carry a load of only twenty-five kilograms — about one jerrycan of kerosene. High winds and bad weather strictly limit the number of days on which sorties can be flown. In fine weather, the helicopters frequently have to fly under fire.

On the higher reaches of the glacier, the soldiers' dependence on the helicopters is absolute. It sometimes happens, a major-general told me, that the men become besotted with these craft and begin to pray to them. This is just one of many species of dementia that come to afflict those who live on the glacier.

Supply problems are particularly acute on the Indian side of the glacier, where the military outposts are separated from their roadheads by long stretches of punishing terrain. Helicopter-time is too precious to be spent on ferrying men between their bases and their posts. Soldiers make their way across the glacier on foot, hefting loads that are often in excess of those carried by Sherpas on Himalayan expeditions. Because of the glacier's constantly-moving surface, each unit must chart its own route. Crevasses appear and disappear in a matter of hours. Some of the posts require a walk of twenty-three days.

'We allow ten extra men per battalion for wastage', an officer told me. Relatively few of the casualties on the glacier are chalked up to hostile fire: the environment imposes a heavier toll on both sides than do the guns of either army. Every year some 1,000 Indian soldiers are believed to sustain injuries on the glacier — about the equivalent of an infantry battalion.

The basic equipment for every Indian soldier on the glacier costs Rs 60,000 — about eleven times what the average Indian can expect to earn in a year. An expert once calculated that every chapati eaten by a Pakistani soldier on the Siachen glacier, bears a cost of about Rs 450 (roughly the average monthly wage for the country).

The Siachen glacier, a senior officer told me, costs India the equivalent of about 20 million US dollars per day: this adds up, in the course of a year, to about one billion dollars — about one-tenth of the country's entire defence budget. Pakistan's costs are much lower but still substantial. The total cost of the Siachen conflict is probably of the same order of magnitude as that of the nuclear programmes of India and Pakistan combined. If the money spent on the glacier were to be divided up and handed out to the people of India and Pakistan, every household in both countries would be able to go out and buy a new cooking stove or a bicycle.

In 1992, there were signs that both countries had reached an agreement on a simultaneous disengagement from Siachen. It was India reportedly that torpedoed the agreement. The diplomats who had negotiated the settlement were told by top politicians: 'A retreat from Siachen will look bad in an election year.' The election came and went leaving the soldiers still at their posts.

We spent a night at a base close to the glacier. In the evening, in the mess, I said to a group of junior officers, 'Do you think the glacier serves any purpose for either country?'

One of the officers laughed. 'You know,' he said, 'once, while climbing an ice face, I asked myself exactly the same thing.'

Another officer added quickly: 'But of course we have to stay.'

'Why?'

'National prestige — this is where India, Pakistan and China meet. We have to hang on, at all costs.'

I was interested to note that Indian soldiers always spoke of their Pakistani counterparts with detachment and respect. Usually they referred to the other side collectively as 'He'; sometimes they used the term *dushman*, 'enemy'. I never once heard any soldier utter a denigratory epithet of any kind.

'Most of us here are from north India', a bluntly spoken major said to me. 'We have more in common with the Pakistanis, if you don't mind my saying so, than we do with South Indians or Bengalis.'

One morning, in a Cheetah helicopter, I followed Fernandes through the gorges that lead up to the glacier. It was cloudy and the brilliant colours of the rockfaces had the blurred quality of a water-washed print. There was a majesty to the landscape the like of which I had never seen before.

We dipped and turned through a sand-braided river valley, trying to make our way up to a post on the glacier. The men at the post, the pilot said, were waiting eagerly for Fernandes. Before him, no Defence Minister had ever thought to pay the glacier a visit.

But the landing was not to be. The cloud-cover was too thick. We headed towards the black, morraine-encrusted snout of the glacier.

Under an open hangar a *burra khana* had been arranged in Fernandes' honour — a kind of feast. Fernandes left the officers' table and began to serve the other ranks, taking the dishes out of the hands of the kitchen staff. The men were visibly moved and so was Fernandes. It was clear that in this job — arrived at fortuitously, late in his career — Fernandes had discovered some kind of vocation, a return perhaps to the remembered austerity and brotherhood of his days as a seminarian or his time as a trade-unionist.

I was introduced to an officer who had just come off the glacier after a three-month tour of duty. He talked proudly of his men and all they had accomplished: injuries had been kept to a minimum, no one had gone mad, they had erected a number of tents and shelters.

He leaned closer. While on the glacier, he said, he'd thought of a plan for winning the war. He wanted to convey it to the Defence Minister. Could I help?

And the plan? I asked.

A nuclear explosion, he explained, inside the glacier, a mile deep. The whole thing would melt and the resulting flood would carry Pakistan away and also put an end to the glacier. 'We can work wonders.'

He'd just come off the glacier, I reminded myself. This was just another kind of altitude sickness.

The next day, sitting in his plane, I talked to Fernandes about Pakistan.

'The soldiers are of the same stock on both sides', he said. 'We cannot win against them and they cannot win against us. Their strength may not be evenly matched against India but their motivation is much greater. This is the reality.'

'Isn't it possible for both sides to disengage from the glacier?' I asked 'Can't some sort of solution be worked out?'

'Does anyone really want a solution?' he said quietly. In his voice there was the same note of despair I'd heard before. 'I don't think anyone wants a solution. Things will just go on, like this.'

Not for the first time, I wondered why Fernandes had taken the risk of bringing me with him. Was it perhaps because he wanted the world to know of his despair and its causes, hoping perhaps that that knowledge would somehow help avert whatever it was that he feared most?

Later, in Pakistan, the defence-affairs specialist, Shirin Mazari, said to me: 'The feeling about Siachen in Pakistan is that we're bleeding India on that front. So let them stay up there for a while and bleed.'

'But Pakistan is bleeding too surely?'

'Not as much as India; they're bleeding more.'

I came to be haunted by this metaphor, because of its undeniable appositeness — its evocation of the vendettas of peasant life along with its reference to the haemorrhaging of lives and resources on the glacier: how better to describe this conflict than through an image of two desperately poor protagonists, balancing upon a barren mountaintop, each with a pickaxe stuck in the other's neck, each propping the other up while waiting for him to bleed to death?

To visit the Siachen glacier is to know that somewhere within the shared collective psyche of India and Pakistan, the torment of an unalterable proximity has given birth to a kind of deathwish, an urge that is rising ever more insistently to the surface.

In Ladakh, during one of our talks, I asked Fernandes what had gone wrong in India. 'The political leadership has refused to break out of its colonial mould', he said. 'The colonial mind stayed on and it allowed the structures of colonial rule to remain. To this day the Collector is the most important person in his area. I am today the Minister of Defence. When I cease to be Minister the Collector in my constituency will not even ask me to sit down. This is the administrative structure the British left behind — a structure that was designed to oppress, exploit and suppress people. Everyone in India knows what the challenges are. But nobody is prepared to stand up and say that these are the challenges and we must face up to them. Nobody is prepared to accept a disciplined life. China went through these challenges and continues to travel that route.'

He told me about a speech he'd made in the Lok Sabha some years ago: he'd pointed at the government benches and said that if India were to deal with corruption the way the Chinese did then everyone sitting there would be shot dead.

The implicit admiration of China seemed ironic to me: just before the tests of 11 May, Fernandes had publicly identified China as India's 'potential enemy number one'. I remarked on this: 'You seem to admire the Chinese; you seem to want India to be more like China.'

'No', he corrected himself. 'Not to be like them — not in terms of their absence of democracy. I am talking about their fight against corruption, in going in for austerity at every level.'

I came to understand that it was not China's institutions or government that were the objects of his admiration, but rather the entirety of its modern experience. 'The Chinese don't have the burden of a colonial military cadre', he said to me once. 'The Chinese army came out of the Long March: the officer-soldier relationship is completely different there. It was experiences like these that formed China and its army. We have never had our Long March.'

In Leh, late one night, sitting in an empty dining-room, Fernandes made the cryptic comment: 'There are no Indians left.'

'What do you mean?'

'There are no Indian parties today. There are only castes and groups gathered around individuals.'

He was referring, I realized, to the increasing frag-mentation of Indian politics and the resulting par-liamentary crises; to the fact that powerful sectional and regional interests have prevented the formation of stable governments over the last few years, pre-cipitating several elections in quick succession. But I remembered also that it was Fernandes himself who was partly responsible for creating the situation that he was now lamenting.

'Do you think,' I asked, 'that some kind of stable party structure might have evolved if you had not resigned in 1977?'

'Yes', he said. 'If the government had survived some sort of national alternative to the Congress might have come about.'

'Do you regret what you did?'

He was unexpectedly frank. 'Yes,' he said, 'I do regret it. And I paid for it very dearly afterwards, in a political sense.'

'Why did you do it?'

'Because of Madhu Limaye', he said, referring to a socialist comrade of his, a well-known political figure of the 1960s and '70s. Limaye had burst into tears one day and implored him to resign. Out of loyalty Fernandes had complied.

This, as Fernandes told it, was the reason why he had brought down a government in which so many millions of his compatriots had invested so much hope.

I began to probe him on his alliance with the Bharatiya Janata Party. 'You were always a secular politician', I said. 'How did you come to link yourself to a religious party?'

In answer Fernandes plunged into history: he spoke of an old political mentor, Ram Manohar Lohia, who had urged him always to be flexible, to maintain a dialogue with every end of the political spectrum. He spoke of a bitter feud with a former protege, Laloo Yadav, a powerful Bihar politician.

Then suddenly he cut himself short. 'Look,' he said, 'I'm rationalizing.'

He had gone to the Bharatiya Janata Party only as a last resort, he explained. He had tried desperately hard to reach agreements with various secular, left-wing parties. None of them would touch him for fear of antagonizing his arch-enemy, Laloo Yadav.

'I tried many doors', he said. 'I went to the BJP only when all other doors were closed. I was facing a wall. There was nowhere else to go.'

The causes of Fernandes' despondency were suddenly blindingly clear. He had spent a lifetime in politics and the system had spun him around and around until what he did and what he believed no longer had the remotest connection. I knew it to be a fact that he still possessed a certain kind of idealism. But what had prevailed finally was vanity, the sheer vanity of power.

Fernandes is not alone in his despondency: there are many others in Indian politics who have a similar — perhaps less acute — sense of being trapped inside a top that is spinning faster and faster while going nowhere. This sense of deadlock is an essential part of the background of the nuclear tests of 11 May: to the leaders of the B.J.P., hanging on to power by the slimmest of parliamentary margins, the tests must have appeared as one means of blasting a way out of a dead end. They had hoped, evidently, to use the tests in building a new political consensus in the country, one that would be centred around their own policies and programmes.

The gambit failed: the tests succeeded only in dividing an already-divided electorate even further. But at the same time, the minority government lost little by staging them and may well have even gained a few more followers. In any event, the costs of the tests — the heightened tension in the region — will not be the B.J.P.'s to pay. For a minority government, there are in effect, no political disincentives for the launching of such gambits.

There is no doubt that the B.J.P. bears the principal responsibility for the tests of 11 May and their consequences. But the blame is not theirs' alone: it was Indira Gandhi and her Congress Party who, in 1974, set the precedent for using nuclear technology as a political spectacle. Since that time many other Indian politicians have battled with the same temptation. Two other recent Indian Prime Ministers, Narasimha Rao and I.K. Gujral, resisted, to their great credit. But it is a matter of public knowledge that they both came very close to succumbing: in slightly different circumstances they might well have done so. In the end, it is in the technology itself that the real danger lies. So long as a nuclear establishment exists it will always provide a temptation to politicians desperate to find ways of keeping a hold on power.

That night in Leh, listening to Fernandes talk I thought of something he had said to me earlier: 'Some day we will sink and this is not anything to do with China or with Pakistan. It is because this country is cursed to put up with a leadership that has chosen to sell it for their own personal aggrandizement.'

This seemed now like a self-indictment — as though he were pointing a finger at himself, in acknowledgement of the fact that he had abandoned all his most dearly-held convictions in embarking on this, the most shameful episode of his career.

S oon after this I flew from New Delhi to Lahore. This was my first visit to Pakistan and the circumstances looked far from propitious. The week before, eighty U.S. Tomahawk missiles had rained down on southern Afghanistan. Some had gone astray and landed south of the border. There was outrage in Pakistan. There were daily reports of Indian and U.S. flags being burned in the streets of Pakistani cities.

At the airport in Lahore, on reaching the end of the immigration queue, I steeled myself for a long wait. My Indian passport would lead, I was sure, to delays, questions, perhaps even an interrogation. But nothing happened: I was waved through with a smile.

When Indians visit Pakistan (and the other way around) there is often an alchemical reaction, a kind of magic. I had heard accounts of this from friends who had been to Pakistan: they had spoken of the warmth, the hospitality, the intensity of emotion, the sense of stepping back into half-recalled memory, the encounters with strangers that began in mid-sentence, like interrupted conversations. Almost instantly upon arrival I found confirmation of these tales — in the smiles that appeared on taxi-drivers' faces, in the stories that people sought me out to tell, in the endless invitations to meals, in the voices of new friends: 'Of course you can't stay in a hotel, what can you be thinking of . . . ?' It was hard to believe that I'd arrived in Lahore knowing no one, armed only with a few telephone numbers.

The tensions of the moment lent an extra dimension of urgency to these new connections. Every morning the papers were filled with news of fresh crises. One morning I opened a Lahore paper, *The News,* to come upon a headline that screamed: '*Pakistan, the idea, is vanishing into thin air*'. The article beneath began: 'Today we are poised at the brink of a historic catastrophe. One can no longer trace even a semblance of method in the madness that characterizes the crisis of the state in Pakistan today.'

I went to see Mr I.A. Rahman, Director of the Human Rights Commission. 'In Pakistan we have never been out of crisis', he told me. 'But this is the worst it's ever been. Everything is discredited, including democracy — in the sense that there has only been a procedural democracy here, a democratic facade.'

Mr Rahman is in his sixties, a member of the generation that came of age before the partition of the subcontinent. 'As a child', he said, 'I had no sense of inferiority towards the developed world. But that has disappeared. Both our countries have been losing ground decade after decade. We have wasted the years of independence.'

One morning I had breakfast with Dr Akmal Hussain, an industrialist and London-trained economist. He explained to me, slowly and patiently, the inevitability of economic collapse. Pakistan had been living wildly beyond its means for many years. The debts had reached a point where they were beginning to outpace the country's revenue. Within a short while the government's entire budget would be spent on two items alone: debt servicing and defence. There would be nothing left for anything else. Because of the Cold War and Pakistan's strategic importance in relation to Afghanistan, these reckless borrowings had been winked and nodded at by the United States. With the end of the Cold War, the nods and winks had ceased abruptly. In May, when India carried out its nuclear tests, Pakistan's economy was already under pressure. When Pakistan responded with its own tests, there was a sudden choking in the lines of credit that had kept the economy alive. The currency plummeted, losing a third of its value in a matter of a few weeks.

Dr Hussain smiled in a melancholy way. 'This may look like a financial crisis', he explained, 'but it is actually a crisis in the real economy. The underlying structure would have caused a meltdown in the long run anyway.' He had predicted all of this years ago, he said, while working as an advisor to the government. No one had paid any attention.

We sat at a table with Dr Hussain's two sons, both school-children, bright energetic boys who were full of questions for their father. He peeled mangoes for them with slow, gentle attentiveness. We drank delicious lassi, made with fresh yogurt. The household's milk came from its own cow, Dr Hussain explained, he'd decided to keep one so the boys could have fresh milk every day. I looked out of the windows. The lawn outside was freshly mown, the garden beautifully laid out.

'I don't think it could get worse', Dr Hussain said. 'This is rock bottom.'

One morning, friends arrived with startling news. The Prime Minister, Mr Nawaz Sharif, had announced his intention to amend the Constitution of Pakistan so that the Shari'a, the corpus of Islamic law, would replace the country's current legal system. This was, my friends said, a development that was just as significant, in its own way, as the nuclear tests of the month of May. If this Amendment went through Parliament everyone's lives would be affected.

I went to see Qazi Hussain Ahmed, the leader of the Jam'aat-e-Islami, the principal religious party in Pakistan. The Jam'aat's Lahore headquarters are on the outskirts of the city, in a large and self-sufficient compound. A high wall surrounds the compound and the entrance is manned by sentries. The buildings inside the complex are of red brick, tastefully designed and well laid out. There are dormitories, educational institutions, residential quarters, health-care facilities, a football field and a large mosque.

A quiet, bearded young man showed me to a well-appointed reception room. Qazi Hussain Ahmed arrived punctually. He had a well-trimmed white beard, twinkling eyes and a manner of great affability. He was dismissive of the proposed constitutional amendment. 'If the Prime Minister really wants to embrace the Shari'a, to embrace Islam,' he said, 'who would block his path? But it's clear that this is a bluff. Instead of using those powers that he already has the Prime Minister wants still more powers. These are all corrupt people. What they've done is loot and pillage and that's what they're still busy doing. The truth is that there is a lot of agitation in the country right now. There is an economic crisis, a political crisis and the government is weak. They know all that. They've done this only to divert attention.'

'What will this crisis do to Pakistan's political institutions?' I asked.

He smiled, his eyes twinkling. 'Other than the army,' he said, 'all the other institutions in this country are more or less finished. Or they have the rattle of death in their throats. And it'll be a good thing when the last breath leaks out of these institutions. These are all feudal institutions, the institutions of a Westernized élite — of people who have made money from them, people who are corrupt. We are now paying the price of their corruption. All the problems we have now — the economic crisis and so on — are the fruit of their corruption.'

At times, while speaking with Qazi Hussain Ahmed, I had a strange intuition of hearing an echo of voices from India. 'We are not for nuclear weapons', he told me, for instance. 'We are ourselves in favour of disarmament. But we don't accept that five nations should have nuclear weapons and others shouldn't. We say, let the five also disarm. If those five want to keep their weapons, then we say others also have a right to do the same. In matters of science, technology and knowledge we cannot accept that any nations have a monopoly.'

On one issue however his views were very different from those I'd heard expressed by politicians in India: the possibility of nuclear war. 'When you have two nations', he said, 'between whom there is so much ill-will, so much enmity as there is between India and Pakistan, and when they both have nuclear weapons, then in the event of war there is always the danger that they would be used. Certainly. In situations of war people become mad. When a nation feels that it is likely to be defeated it can do anything to spare itself the shame.'

The word crisis was on everyone's lips. Yet the rooms in which it was spoken were invariably neat, well-appointed, filled with books, paintings, vases, lamps — all the usual accoutrements of well-ordered lives. I took to glancing out of windows at the mention of the word — looking, as it were, for visual confirmation outside. But almost invariably the streets were just as orderly as the interiors of the houses I was visiting. The traffic was much better regulated than New Delhi's and destitution was much less in evidence; the pavements were cleaner, the air infinitely more fresh. There was nothing frenetic in the comportment of pedestrians and passersby: on the contrary they seemed to possess more than their proper share of old-world grace. Where then was the crisis that everyone spoke of, the historic catastrophe? People assured me that it was all around us. At dinner tables there were arguments about how long it would be before Taliban-like groups made a bid for power. After dessert, the talk would turn to the buying of Kalashnikovs. At every meal there was a sense that the winds whipping at the tablecloth were the first blasts of a gathering gale.

I came to realize that I was looking for the wrong signs.

So persuasive is the metaphor of the state as architectural edifice, that when we think of one succumbing to a crisis, it is inevitably in images of collapse: of a sudden caving in, an explosion, black clouds of debris rising high to obscure the sun of normalcy. This is a misleading image: we should think instead of water leaching out of a lake — a process that is slow, indeterminate, muddy, unclear. In some seasons the flow appears to reverse itself; inexplicably the waters rise, gloom is dispelled, but only to gather again, in even greater force, when the level dips once again.

The bed of a parched lake is neither level nor dead. It is dotted with anthills, tree trunks, rocks; here and there islands and outcrops remain, soaring above their surroundings. This is an ecological niche that is peculiar to itself and the process of its creation is neither apocalyptic nor wholly destructive. As the waters of the lake seep slowly away, it becomes clear that everything is not to be swept away, as, for instance, in a flood; on the contrary, certain features that had lain hidden beneath the water's surface, are revealed to possess an unexpected strength; others achieve a new salience. Armies, for example, become stronger, better organized, more single-minded in their purpose; the enclaves of the rich and the criminal become fortresses, defended by high walls and private armies; certain kinds of voluntary organizations, religious groupings, and so on flourish as never before. These entities recreate for themselves some of the services that were once offered by the state: telephones, policing, basic healthcare, education, the generation of electricity; perhaps even the supply of water. What is lost principally is that life-giving element that once provided the lake's varied features with a linking commonality. But even on the cracked

and dust-blown bed of the vanished lake, all is
not lost — just beneath the parched surface, pockets
of moisture remain, breeding, from season to season,
small patches of reeds and grass and the occasional
stunted bush. Perhaps one day — who knows? —
these remnants may succeed in attracting water
back into the lake.

This is not a lonely road and Pakistan is far from
being the only subcontinental nation that stands
wavering at its fork.

If there was any one person I wanted to meet in
Lahore, it was Asma Jahangir, Pakistan's leading
human rights lawyer and a figure of legend among
democratic activists everywhere. I'd followed her
career for years: I'd read about her defence of the
rights of religious minorities; her work on behalf of
women; her dogged interrogation of Pakistan blasphemy laws; her refusal to cave in, either to govern-
mental pressure or to fundamentalist death threats.
So far as I am concerned Asma Jahangir ranks with
Burma's Aung San Suu Kyi as a figure of moral
authority and an embodiment of courage.

One evening I found myself at a dinner party
where Asma was expected. She'd been held up in
court, her husband said; she was holding discussions
with other lawyers about the proposed constitutional
amendment. It was about ten when Asma finally

arrived. Two Kalashnikov-toting bodyguards walked her to the door and took up positions outside. It was explained to me that she cannot go anywhere except under heavy guard.

A moment before someone had said: 'If you put Asma on one side and a million men on the other, there would be no doubt about who would win — Asma.' Not without reason, I had expected someone larger than life. But she proved instead to be a slim, diminutive woman with the crackling intensity of a high-tension cable. Her voice was that of someone many times her size: it was a beautiful voice, smoky, richly textured, but with a sharply abrasive edge.

Through much of that evening she held us spell-bound, with stories about the courts and about her cases. Later — as so often in Pakistan — the conversation turned to the question of when the Taliban would begin to play a decisive role in Pakistan — not 'whether', I couldn't help noting, but 'when'. Asma spoke with great eloquence on this subject. Her position (as she was to describe it to me later) was this: 'If the Taliban win we are in trouble; if the Taliban lose we are in trouble. If they win control of Afghanistan, our policies will have to be influenced because we are trying to get to the Central Asian republics and we will have to have that inter--action with the government [in Afghanistan]. Plus the fact that the Taliban are Pakhtoons and they are sitting in the North-West Frontier Province. We have a porous border with Afghanistan; the Taliban's interest is to keep it porous. Already you can see [their] influence in the North-West Frontier Province and Peshawar. And if they lose the war — a large number of the Taliban come from Pakistan as you've seen [in the recent American bombings of Bin Laden's camp in Afghanistan] — they will obviously come back [here] and they will bring back the comrades who have fought with them. These are going to be unemployed, desperate people with an agenda [of their own]. How are they going to amalgamate in this society? It is difficult for me to see. When you begin to convince yourself that you're doing this for your religion and for God, it becomes even more dangerous, because then you are a desperado. The Taliban are very well armed and trained. They have ideology on their minds and [they are] used to power. No jobs, no future. Will the Government of Pakistan be able to contain these people? The Government of Pakistan will be very dependent on the army, which is the only organized force that could contain the Taliban. I don't know how long it would be before the army started having friction [within itself]. This is something I cannot predict.'

The others who were present varied in their estimation of how long it would take for the Taliban to substantially infiltrate Pakistani politics. But their guesses were not far apart; they ranged from two years to ten. It was clear that this eventuality, if it ever came to pass, would spell disaster for almost everyone in that room. Yet there was nothing portentous about this conversation. Indeed, perhaps the most alarming aspect of it was its measured and confident realism.

I was struck by this: it seemed to me illustrative of one of the striking differences between India and Pakistan, especially where the nuclear debate is concerned. In India it is no easy matter to persuade people that nuclear weapons constitute a real and pressing threat. The prevalent attitude among Indian nuclearists is that the worst has never happened and so it never will — and if it did the last place it would happen in is India. It is as though the very idea of historic danger were abstract and insubstantial, a red herring dangled by those who seek to deny India her rightful place in the world. In Pakistan on the other hand, the idea of historic catastrophe appears not in the least unreal: the country has been circling the eyes of storms for decades, almost without interruption. This, I think, is why the nuclear discussion has much more a tone of realism there than in India, much more a sense that the subject at hand concerns the here and now.

In this assymetry of perceptions there lies a real danger. Indian nuclearists seem to believe, in many cases sincerely, that they are merely running laps in a race for prestige — one that is not much different from the contest of the Olympic Games. They believe that they and their Pakistani counterparts are essentially in agreement on the nature of the game and the rules that regulate it.

But in Pakistan nuclear weapons are not perceived
in the same way that they are in India: they cannot
be. One of the most devastating conflicts of our era
has been — is being — waged on Pakistan's thresh-
old. Ordinary Pakistanis are well aware that their
country is slowly falling victim to this conflict. Pakistanis know full well the difference between weapons
and icons. They see nuclear weapons as instruments
of mass destruction that pose a whole range of threats
— ranging from political intimidation and blackmail,
to the possibility of annihilation. From these perceptions, people of different inclinations draw different lessons. For many — including Asma and
other like-minded Pakistanis — the lesson is that
these weapons must be done away with at once,
unilaterally if need be. But there are others who use
the same perceptions to arrive at conclusions of a
completely different kind.

In India I met very few people — including anti-
nuclear activists — who believed that a nuclear war
might actually occur in the subcontinent. In Pakistan,
the opposite was true: almost everyone I met thought
that nuclear war almost certainly lay head, somewhere
down the road. I came to be convinced that Indian
nuclearists are utterly in error in their belief that their
Pakistani counterparts share their own bland assump-
tions about nuclear weaponry. There is an abyss here
— a gap of perception — of which both sides are
dangerously unaware. Unfortunately, a nuclear stand-
off is the only known circumstance in which very

small divergences of attitude and response can lead to millions of deaths.

Dr Durrsameem Ahmed, a Lahore psychologist, with many friends in India, said to me one day: 'I see Pakistan as a male child trying to detach itself from its maternal matrix. India is the devouring mother trying to consume its own child. It's a mutual obsession between mother and son and psychology is full of it. If they don't let go they will destroy each other. It would seem that the possibility was there from the start, with Kashmir as the serpent in the paradise of independence. Nuclear war is not just likely. I would say there is a certain inevitability to it. Frankly I am terrified: terror is an understatement.'

A few days later, a friend arranged for me to talk to Asma Jahangir at length. It so happened that that very morning the Pakistan government had issued a circular listing the names of the three people whose lives were believed to be most at risk: Asma's was one of them. On reading the item, I'd tried to imagine what her response would be: alarm, I thought, would be the very least of it. But I discovered that I was wrong — in fact, Asma hadn't so much as bothered to read the article.

'I should make it clear', Asma said, 'that I enjoy what I do and death threats are a part of the work.

It's not something you don't foresee. I've had attacks on my person; I've had people coming into my mother's house to kill me. They've taken my brother and his family hostage. I've had a man arrested from the courtroom with a gun; I've had my car broken by a mob [while defending a Christian] in a blasphemy case; I've had other death threats — like slogans written on buses, saying "kill her, we are your *maut* [death] Asma Jahangir".'

'Doesn't this frighten you?'

'To be very honest, when my mother's house was attacked and my brother and his wife and my nephew were taken hostage it really did frighten me. I met those who came to kill me subsequently in the police station and they were filled with venom against me.'

'What was this based on?'

'They actually believed that I was some kind of demon. They believed that by defending a case of blasphemy I was encouraging blasphemy against the Holy Prophet. [They believed] that I stood against all decent norms. That I was a kind of devil incarnated that would wreck the whole social fabric of Pakistan.'

'What was it like to meet them?'

'It was strange. First of all they had a very different impression of what I was like, even visually. Slowly and gradually, as the ice was broken it became clear that this perception had been given to them by some mullahs, preaching in the mosque, by two or three lawyers, by one newspaper. They thought I wanted women to become *behaya* [licentious] and once this happened they would have no control over their sisters and mothers. [But after the meeting] they got bail and turned up at my office with some sweetmeats and wanted me to have them. I couldn't because here were men who wanted not only to kill me, but to kill my sister and my children as well. And that they should want me to have sweets after they got bail was, I think, a bit crude on their part.'

She laughed uproariously, and then went on to add: 'A few months ago I was in court and this young man comes up to me and complains — you are a human rights person but our case is not getting anywhere and can't you do anything about it? Suddenly I saw that this was one of the men who'd come to kill me. And he was complaining to me about his own trial — where I was the complainant! I was quite taken aback and I said to him, in Punjabi, *"nale chot ta nale chattar: ja apna case aap kar"* [go and fight your own case].'

We laughed. 'Tell me about your formative years', I said. 'How did you become a human rights activist?' 'I was born in 1952,' she said, 'I went to school here, and then to Kinnaird College [in Lahore]. I took my law degree here. I am completely indigenous. I was born in a household where my father was in politics and he was always in the opposition. And so I have seen him go in and out of jail. He was one of the few West Pakistanis who were from the Awami League [otherwise the League's support came mainly from East Pakistan]. So one has seen that whole aspect of what is treason and what is a traitor as compared with people's basic rights. During the [Bangladesh] war and before that he was in jail for many years. During Ayub Khan's time he was in jail for many years. When I was a teenager I used to look after a number of things when he was in jail — my mother couldn't do everything and we didn't have a political party to fall back on. It was at the end of Ayub Khan's period that I got really motivated. I began as a campaigner when I organized a procession of women during Ayub Khan's time — that was my first public exposure as such. And then my father went to jail during Yahya Khan's period. He was released but the first day Mr Bhutto came to power he arrested him again. I had just turned eighteen at that time and I filed a petition against his arrest which became a very celebrated case in India and Pakistan. It changed constitutional history because it was the first case that said that a military intervention is unconstitutional. The case started in 1970 but the judgement was in 1972. They declared Yahya Khan's government illegal and consequently the martial law orders under which my father was arrested were also illegal. So they released him. This made me very interested in law because I was very much involved in that case as a petitioner. And the lawyers were very kind to me. I was all of eighteen but they used to tell me what the arguments were. By this time my father was under house arrest and I had to go back [home] and tell him what happened. And if I didn't answer his questions properly he would get very frustrated because he wanted to know the arguments. Plus, even before that, my father used to be in jails outside of Lahore and he never wanted us to come and meet him there. Only when he was called to court in Lahore did we children see him. So for me the courts became a place where you met your father and where justice was given out. I made up my mind to be a lawyer. At that time I thought it was a haven for justice. Where the rule of law was upheld. It was only after I became a lawyer that I realized how it was upheld.'

'But it hasn't diminished your idealism?' I said.

'It has absolutely diminished my idealism', Asma replied. 'To the extent that this was not idealism — I was just misinformed. I don't think there is any such thing as the rule of law that is being upheld by the courts of Pakistan. I have no misconception about that at all. But I still think that these institutions are made with our money and we have to keep knocking. Every knock must be a knock at their conscience. And we must keep knocking and keep knocking until their conscience responds . . . I am not an idealist at all. I am a very practical person. You need [to choose] the right case. You need the right bench. You need the right timing. You [should have] groomed public opinion before [taking the case]. An activist must never be an idealist. They must be very practical and they must strategize each part of their actions. Particularly in the courts. Because once you get a judgment from the Supreme Court, it takes perhaps half a generation to get it overturned.'

I asked: 'What will happen if this proposed constitutional amendment — the fifteenth amendment, instituting the Shari'a — is passed?'

'Well,' she said, 'first of all it will mean that I'll be out of a brief. Because the ordinary law will not work. I will have to argue my case, every case, in terms of Islamization. Secondly, fundamental rights will be redefined. We will not have an independent judiciary. Any judge that does not toe the government line will be sent home because he will fall under the definition of state functionary. And the constitutional amendment says that any state functionary who is seen to be doing wrong according to the directives of the government can be sent home. So I will really be arguing before a judiciary that will already be told by the government what judgment to give. Then [there is] the whole question of the small provinces and provincial government. If the federal government is going to give the directives of what is wrong and what is right then they [the provincial governments] will become dummies. I'm not saying we have a marvellous legal system at the moment. We have a very mediocre legal system. But that will be the end of it. I would not wish to practice in that legal system.'

I said: 'What exactly is the sort of Islamic legal

system that is envisaged as being put in place? Is it to be Sunni law and, if so, which school of practice will it follow — Maliki or Hanafi or Shafi'i or what?'

Asma nodded: 'Absolutely. The proposed amendment says that every sect can interpret it for themselves, which really means also planting sectarianism. If I am a Maliki and I'm married to someone who is Shafi'i then what personal law will apply? Mine or his? Or if I have a contract? [What] if I'm a Sunni and I have a contract with a Shi'a? It'll be pure confusion — it'll be a free-for-all; it'll create havoc for the legal system. Also, despite the fact that the fifteenth amendment has two lines saying that the rights of minorities will not be disturbed, every minority group has taken a stand against it. And the government has tried every card, you know. [They've said] people are anti-religious if they oppose it; [they've said] people are siding with Vajpayee [and the B.J.P.] if they oppose it. Well, I think anyone who proposes orthodox Islam in Pakistan is actually strengthening the hands of the [B.J.P.].'

'In what way?'

'In the sense that fanaticism here brings fanaticism in India. It has a snowball effect and a reaction. In 1985 we had a conference in Delhi. One of the Indian ministers — Margaret Alva — was chairing the meeting. I had read a paper on Zia's Islamization and how it had affected the lives of women in Pakistan. She was quite happy. She was almost smirking. She asked me a few questions from the chair, sounding very surprised, smirking a little. Afterwards I said this to her, I said: "You know, don't look so comfortable because what happens in our country will soon catch up here [in India]. Then we will [both] over-react once again".'

'You're right', I said. 'And from what you're saying about the fifteenth amendment, it sounds as though it could cause the legal system to collapse.'

Asma's answer was categorical: 'It will collapse. The legal system will collapse, the judiciary will collapse. [We will be left] to the dictates of a handful of people.'

I asked: 'What is the future of the Mohajir movement in Sind?'

She said: 'Let me say this — and there have been reports of the Human Rights Commission saying the same thing — every ethnic group has the right to make demands. You may disagree with them and say that they want more than their fair share. But disagreement has to be intellectual and it has to be through dialogue. The fact that we resist a movement to start with and begin with the lowest kind of attack on their integrity, tends to harden the situation. I or you may believe that this movement was put up; we may believe that this was a terrorist movement, but the responsibility of the government is to engage in dialogue, not to start dubbing them one thing or another. In every movement there are all kinds of people, and you want to bring a dialogue forward in order to encourage those people who want a peaceful settlement. I think there has not been enough reaching out. You can't kill a movement through state terrorism, if I may use that word, because then you're really strengthening the movement.'

I said: 'Travelling in Pakistan over the last few days, I have a sense of impending crisis, really deep crisis. Do you think I'm wrong?'

'Well,' she retorted, 'I cannot recall any one month when Pakistan has not gone from crisis to crisis — and I mean from way back, from the 1960s up to now. But at that time [in the 1960s] the crisis was more related to domestic politics and it didn't seem as though it was going to be insurmountable.'

'Would you say that what has happened in Pakistan is the result of having a very small ruling class?'

She said: 'A ruling élite that is devoid of all values, which gives leadership only to the agenda that everybody is for themselves — that is the disaster of Pakistan. If you look at the ruling classes of Pakistan and compare them to the ruling classes of India, Sri Lanka, Bangladesh and Nepal, you will find very few people who are actually worried, who are actually taking an interest, who actually interact with the people of this country. They live like foreigners here. And that is I think the unfortunate part. Most of the ruling classes of Pakistan have always sided with the establishment. The few exceptions are freaks really. Even Mr Bhutto was from the establishment. If you look at it that way, it's pathetic.'

I asked: 'What would you say needs to be changed?'

'First of all, the intrusion of religion and religious orthodoxy into the politics of Pakistan. This has never been resolved; there were always strange compromises. Secondly, the whole question of provincial autonomy [needs to be addressed]. This has hounded Pakistan's politics, even to the extent of having lost one part of Pakistan because of the majority-empowered province's mentality of trying to push their decisions on others. Previously these issues were sort of muffled, or they had not come to the surface because there was always a dictatorship and the smaller provinces were threatened with being called traitors if they said anything against the federation or the power of the federation. With the democratic process — and I must give credit to the Press particularly — people have begun to speak up and a debate has been generated.

'The added problem is that Pakistan's foreign policy was central to the Cold War. We have still not mentally reconciled ourselves, as a nation, to the post-Cold War scenario. We cannot think that we'll make mistakes and somebody will come to our rescue. These rescue operations have finished, and that is something we have still not comprehended fairly and squarely. There comes a time when the world focuses on changes and people begin to leave you to your own devices.'

I said: 'I have the sense that there is a very powerful groundswell of anti-Western sentiment here. Yet Pakistan was a close Western ally for much of the last half-century. How does one account for this?'

Asma replied: 'The Americans supported Zia ul-Haq, who was one of the most ruthless dictators in our part of the world. They supported his Islamization process until the American people woke up to what he was doing to women. When Zia ul-Haq came to power he was completely backed by the Americans to back the jihad in Afghanistan. The American Centre used to send scholars to lecture us on this. To the extent that we've heard lectures where [American] scholars have told us how great Saudi Arabian society was, and that women could operate within their own sphere of life. After a while people said, well, if it's such a great and romantic system, perhaps the United States needs to import it themselves.'

She continued: 'At that time we did not have that violent a society where Kalashnikovs were easily available and we did not have a rampant drug culture in our country. This all started with the Afghan war and the jihad. And this so-called jihad did create a very strong network of orthodoxy in our country and we are still suffering under that. So even liberals

are a little bitter at the fact that these problems
were created by the West. I'm not saying that one
can rest on the premise that it's the West that creates
problems, and that it's the West that can do away
with our problems. We are to blame for our own
follies. Except that in the case of Zia ul-Haq, it
was not as though people here weren't struggling
against him. Several people got flogged, including
lawyers. Several people got executed — even boys
as young as fifteen. People went to jail. I do not
recall any of my colleagues in the Human Rights
Commission who did not go to jail at that time.
[But at the same time] people like us are not happy
with West-bashing. The Islamists are very militant
against the West because they feel that the US
picked them up, they made them into the custodians
of the country and now they're backing off. So they
feel let down on another level. They continue West-
bashing to the point where they dub people like
myself as Western agents, having conveniently forgotten that ten years ago they were the ones who
were the direct beneficiaries of the jihad policy of
the West.'

I changed the subject: 'In what way do you think
the Kashmir issue could be settled between India and
Pakistan?'

'Frankly', she began, 'I don't think the two governments are sincere about settling the issue. On
the one hand, it's a complicated issue whether Pakistan should be interfering or not. Pakistan gives the

example of Bangladesh, where people were really being oppressed and were going to lose many lives. If the Government of Pakistan were to intervene I would be happier; I am not happy at the idea of vigilantes intervening. It's like me putting up an army and saying I want to fight a war in Bosnia. The answer I get to that is, no, Bosnia is not a disputed territory and Kashmir is. But let the Government of Pakistan be in charge of what they are doing there. At the same time I have read, particularly in the past two, three years, a number of reports, even by the Indian NGOs about the kind of intervention the [Indian] army has had in the Valley, and you cannot expect people not to be antagonistic — the number of people that have been killed, the number of women that have been raped. These are not exaggerated figures, because they have come from Indian NGOs themselves. Unless those people themselves are in the process of dialogue you will not be able to have a long-lasting solution there. Because let us even presume that tomorrow India and Pakistan for whatever reason decide the issue — it will not be closed. The issue will come up time and again unless there is an interaction with the leaders of the Kashmiri movement themselves. And perhaps the question then is, who are the genuine leaders? A mechanism ought to be put in place — certainly not without India and Pakistan — to ascertain who are the genuine leaders there. In the process even the Kashmiris' own perceptions of where they want to go may change. When people are confronted [with such a situation] then the rhetoric finishes. Then it is reality [that they are dealing with] and in a situation of [confronting] reality they may take a very, very different stance.'

The first part of her answer had seemed to me so uncannily reminiscent of what George Fernandes had said to me a few days earlier that I wanted to hear more. I asked: 'You just said that the leaders in the two countries are not interested in solving the problem. What exactly do you mean by that?'

'In our country', she said, 'we feel that if we solve the situation with anything short of having Kashmir with us it will be very unpopular with the people of Pakistan because of the high profile that we have given this issue and because of the rhetoric that we have had. But frankly it is not within Pakistan's power to have both sides of Kashmir [with it] — even the Kashmiris may not agree with that. So who wants to take that risk? [Especially] after the expectations of people have been raised that Kashmir will be a part of Pakistan? Similarly on the part of the Indians. The Indian government will not wish to see any part of Kashmir leave India's hands or even go into neutral hands. And that is a risk they will have to take if they want to come to talks and say, okay, these talks are for a solution. It's a messy situation where the governments don't have the courage, the confidence, or the moral conviction to face the realities.'

'Would you say then', I asked, 'that Kashmir is the principal problem between India and Pakistan? Or would problems remain even without Kashmir?'

She said: 'I think if the Kashmir issue is solved tomorrow we would still have problems: we would have problems on our water disputes; we would have problems on our influence in the region. India is a very large country. India has political ambitions in the region. Ours is a smaller country, but because of our past history of being aligned with the U.S.A. and the policies we have had a hand in, we have got used to having an influence. We've got used to a strategy where we like to be seen as a very influential country. Then there is a problem of perception. India wants to push a perception of South Asian identity; Pakistan wants a South Asian identity and yet does not want it. It wants to leave the door open to an identity as a Middle Eastern country. So I think even in terms of foreign policy there will be friction; in terms of hegemony in South Asia there will be friction. India unfortunately in the past has annoyed many of its neighbours. If Pakistan tomorrow has a more reasonable leadership, a leadership that is looking toward South Asia as an identity, they have the possibility of more or less isolating India, which is going to make India very unhappy. So that historical animosity is not going to go away that quickly. That will only go when both countries recognize each other's strength instead of trying to exploit each other's weaknesses. The last point which is very important is that we have a large Muslim minority in India. And you have Hindus in Pakistan. And the question of minorities will always remain on the agenda of India and Pakistan. When the Muslims in Bombay are hit, it hurts the Muslims in Pakistan; when the Hindus in Sindh are persecuted it annoys India. So that again will be a point of friction. If there is keen interest in ending this animosity — and I would say this is very much linked with the Kashmir issue — both countries' leadership must sign an accord protecting minorities.'

I came at last to the nuclear issue: 'What was your response when you woke up on 11 May and read about the nuclear blasts?'

Her voice slowed. 'After the Indian tests a debate was going on, on whether Pakistan should react in a similar fashion or not. A few of us at that time took the stand that we should not react by testing a nuclear bomb. And there are reasons: one is that we should de-link our foreign policy from India. We cannot have a foreign policy just in reaction to India. Secondly we felt that Pakistan was not going to gain anything by a test; that this was a good opportunity for us to go a separate way completely. Pakistan should have taken the moral high ground at that point. Frankly if I had had anything to do with decision-making, I would have said, let us take the moral high ground now. If I had anything to do with the leadership of Pakistan I would have gone first of all to Tokyo

and led a huge procession against nuclearization;
I would have gone to Ireland and led a procession
against nuclearization. Everywhere in the major
capitals of the world you would have got strong
support and it would really have decimated India's
image in many ways and brought Pakistan an
image in the international community as a far
more reasonable country. And a leadership can
always control domestic opinion, particularly in our
countries. And the people of our countries —
India, Pakistan, Bangladesh — are very wise in
their perceptions. If you show them how this issue
is linked to their little kitchen at home, they
understand it. There are always a few handfuls of
people who are gung-ho; who would distributes
sweets. But the same people who distributed sweets
in India and Pakistan [at the time of the nuclear
tests] are the same people who would come out
and riot if they saw an economic crunch. Look at
the education of our people in terms of what a
nuclear bomb is. If we knew what a nuclear bomb
was we wouldn't have people on the road dis-
tributing sweetmeats. We wouldn't have people
celebrating and dancing. They think that it's a
kite-flying contest, like an India-Pakistan bokaata:
it's a really amazing and frightening reaction. To
take that kind of extreme public opinion [into
account] in deciding the life of a nation, is not
wise leadership.'

I asked: 'When these blasts happened in Pokharan,

did you feel that they were an act of hostility directed at Pakistan?'

'Well frankly, I felt angry. I felt angry at the Indian leadership because I felt that they were going to start a nuclear race in the region. And yes, I felt that my security was threatened. But I [also] felt: if we do the same it'll be doubly threatened. I have never felt so insecure, so unhappy in my life as [I was] after we tested our own nuclear device. I felt doubly insecure. I am not convinced of the argument that it is a deterrent.'

'Do you feel that a nuclear war is a possibility?'

She said: 'If you ask me, anything is a possibility between India and Pakistan. Because our policies are irrational. Our decision-making is ad hoc. We have been surrounded by disinformation about each other. We have a historical enmity. We have this whole emotionalism of jihad against each other — on our part it is jihad; on your part there is a lobby that will never accept the existence of Pakistan. We are fatalistic nations who believe that whatever has happened — famine, accidents, drought — it is the will of God. We learn to accept every catastrophe. Our decision-making is done by a few opinion makers on both sides. It's not the ordinary woman living in a village in Bihar whose voice is going to be heard, who is going to say, for God's sake I don't want this nuclear bomb, I want my cow and milk for my children. She is nowhere, she doesn't figure anywhere. It worries me. It really worries me.'

'But despite all this', I said, 'I know that you've been involved in reaching out to India, in people-to-people contacts. What is it that keeps you interested in doing that?'

'Because', she said, 'I have a great faith in people's own instincts. I can give you a recent example — of two young colleagues from my office, two young chaps, lawyers, who went to India and who've just come back. They were amazed. I've been there myself, so I could relate. They said, "we went into temples, nobody stopped us!" One young chap was staying with a Hindu family who had moved during Partition. These were two people who were not aware: who had less trust in what I was saying than in Pakistan television's propaganda. So they came back really amazed. They said, "We went to the Supreme Court, and they knew about laws passed in Pakistan! There were people who were very worried about our country!" And the language, the cultural habits, the body language. All of that is very much alike, particularly when you talk about Delhi and Lahore — there is far less difference than between Lahore and Quetta. I think once you break the barriers of disinformation, people's own instincts are what we have to depend on. I feel hopeful.'

My stay in Pakistan ended with a visit to the Wagah border post. Wagah is, of course, the only official crossing-point between India and Pakistan: it is also the locale for the climactic scene in Sa'adat Hassan Manto's wonderful story, *Toba Tek Singh*. I'd heard about the ritual that takes place at Wagah every day at sunset when the flags of India and Pakistan are lowered: I was keen to see it for myself.

I went to Wagah with a group of actors from a Lahore-based company called the Ajoka Public Theatre. This troupe is headed by the well-known activist and director, Madiha Gauhar, and her playwright husband, Shahid Nadeem. Its members are young — mainly in their twenties and thirties — and they are drawn from widely varied backgrounds: some make a modest living working in shops and government offices, while others come from Lahore's élite. Their plays are political in content and are often performed in streetcorners and other public places. Their rehearsals are usually conducted on the open roof of their Lahore office, under the astonished gaze of their neighbours. But despite severe limitations of space and money, their productions are sophisticated, well-acted and crisply staged: Ajoka has a devoted following among theatre aficionados in India as well as Pakistan.

We went in a small car — the Pakistani equivalent of an Indian Maruti-Suzuki (these cars I discovered were just as ubiquitous in Pakistan as they are in India). Four members of the Ajoka Theatre accompanied me on this expedition, three men and one woman. This last was the tall and strikingly beautiful Savera, who is both a serious actress and a popular television star.

This was not the first time my companions had made the journey to Wagah. Over the last several years the border post has become a pilgrimage for Indian and Pakistani peace activists. On New Year's Eve groups from both sides of the border converge at this point. This has become a yearly ritual, an annually recurring moment when the subcontinent's peoples are able to snatch an instant of sanity from their rulers' maw.

The year before (1997) several members of the Ajoka Theatre had joined in the annual Wagah pilgrimage. The ceremony had taken a strange turn. Because of the active discouragement of the Pakistan government, the organizers had assumed that the turnout would be low. But just before New Year's Eve, word spread that the Bombay filmstar, Shahrukh Khan, would be accompanying the Indian contingent. Legion is Shahrukh Khan's following in Pakistan. Busloads of frenzied fans descended on Wagah. Shrieking teenage girls rendered inaudible the measured utterances of peace activists. But then, alas, it came to be known that the advent of the awaited hero was not to be: that the Shahrukh Khan story was nothing more than rumour, a filmic chimera. Pandemonium ensued. The police descended in a whirlwind of flailing batons. All the men present were bundled up and carried away, like so many pelts from a hunt. Women, on the other hand, were allowed into the walled sanctum where the steel gates of nationhood frown at each other across a paved stretch of no-man's land. But no sooner had they encountered their counterparts from across the border, than the police descended once again to tear them apart, fans and activists alike. The year had not begun well for the peacefully-inclined

The drive to Wagah was a short one, through countryside that was even more lush and green than that on the other side of the Punjab border. We passed through towns that still bore traces of the Indian army's inland march in the 1965 war. As they pointed out the sights, my companions sang old Hindi film-songs, *'beqaraar karke hame yun na jaayiye . . .'* It so happened that the Ajoka Theatre's principal singer was with us: his renditions were astonishingly good, unmarred even by the drumming of the car.

On reaching the walls of the Wagah post, Savera was immediately set upon by fans. We tore her away and made our way into the inner sanctum. There was a tall gate, flanked by viewing galleries. The galleries were filled with people. There were a good number of Pakistanis present, mostly women, many of them dressed in black burqas. But for the most part the audience consisted of Japanese tourists, scrubbed and pastel-clothed, and armed with electronic arsenals.

A great buzzing of video cameras signalled the

start of the main event. Black-uniformed border guards appeared, in the midst of a tumult of barked commands. The guards were all of formidable size, well over six feet tall, and their height was emphasized by their enormous black turbans. I was put in mind of a basketball team at a fancy dress ball. Later, I was informed that both armies reserve their tallest and most imposing-looking men for these border squads.

Leading the squad was an immense turbaned soldier with a reddish, henna-stained moustache. He went goose-stepping to the gates and flung them open, to reveal an equally tall, equally well moustachioed Indian soldier doing exactly the same thing, a few feet away. The two men snapped to attention, their chests all-but-touching, frowning fiercely into each other's faces. Then, standing inches apart, they launched upon a series of complicated drill manoeuvres, strutting and preening and stamping their feet like anxious roosters. Their steps were perfectly coordinated on both sides, every movement being enacted in perfect unison. It was clear, from the rehearsed precision of their performance, that they spent just as much time in synchronizing the rhythms of their limbs as do most honeymooning newlyweds. Yet, their faces were frozen into masks of snarling ferocity and their eyes flashed defiance as brightly as those of Kathakali dancers. There was something so sublimely comic in this pantomime that even the Japanese tourists were moved to laughter.

Then the flags were lowered, crossing each other in exactly symmetrical lines of descent. Red Moustache came strutting back towards the galleries. Through the corner of his mouth he hissed at the audience: *'Naara-e-Hydari!'*. Dutifully, a few voices cried out, 'Allahu Akbar'. After a moment's hesitation, several Japanese tourists joined in. There was some confusion between 'r's and 'l's. Red Moustache seemed none too pleased.

In the distance, on the far side of the border, great numbers of people stood gathered in a gallery, not unlike ours. Interspersed among a mass of dhotis and sarees, we could see the electric pastels of yet another contingent of Japanese tourists. They were gazing curiously in our direction, from my homeland.

In response to the *Naara-e-Hydari* we heard the crowd on the far side give voice to the cry: 'Bharat Mata ki jai.' This caused confusion among the tourists on our side; some of them got their slogans mixed up and shouted, tremulously, ' . . . ki jai, . . . ki jai'. This invited fierce frowns from Red Moustache.

Then the great steel gates swung shut on creaking hinges and the Japanese tourists filed quietly away, back towards their airconditioned buses. A few small knots of people remained in the galleries, all of them Pakistani, most of them women. Suddenly a ripple went through these remnants of the crowd and people went surging forward, the burqa-clad women leading the way. A small tongue of unwalled space extended into no-man's land, like a ship's bowsprit.

We went rushing into this space, and then froze, finding ourselves almost face-to-face with an exactly similar group from the other side. People stood where they were and stared, I at my compatriots, they at us. The tall barbed-wire fence that marks the border was close at hand. It stretched away into the distance, through the lush green fields.

Nobody said anything: everyone stood and stared. A couple of women tried to wave, and were spotted by Red Moustache. 'No waving!' he snapped. The hands fell back. A couple of women wandered too close to the far side. The guards fell upon them and dragged them away.

Then suddenly Savera was recognized. The border was instantly forgotten: the world of the screen became a reminder of real life.

We rescued Savera and made our way slowly back towards our parked car. Red Moustache approached us, smiling widely. Unbending after the effort of his labours, he stooped stiffly from his great height, to enquire after the telephone number of a member of our group. The others burst into rollicking laughter and slapped their comrade on his back: 'Careful — you know what *he* wants.'

We got into our car and drove away, still laughing, but at nothing in particular. We were all, I think, a little awestruck by the perfection of the enactment we had just witnessed: this precisely performed staging of a parodic enmity, produced by unseen regimes, and directed by Red Moustache and his ilk. It was as though we were in one of those cartoon-film situations where a train filled with looney-tune characters is heading towards a precipice — a chasm that is clearly visible to the audience and concealed only from the protagonists. On screen, as in real life, this predicament never fails to raise a laugh.

There is every reason to fear a nuclear catastrophe in South Asia.

Both India and Pakistan have ballistic missiles. Both countries are capable of hitting several of each other's major cities. Because of the limited resources of both countries, the production and storage of nuclear warheads will necessarily have to be concentrated in a few facilities. India's current nuclear weapons' production, for instance, is thought to be concentrated in a single unit: the Bhabha Atomic Research Centre in Bombay. Both sides can therefore realistically hope to destroy each other's production and storage capacities with a single strike.

It is very unlikely that either side contemplates launching such an assault. But at the same time they both have to be prepared to respond in the event of facing such an attack themselves. In other words, to deter a first strike, they have to be prepared to launch a counter-strike.

Several major cities in India and Pakistan are within a few hundred miles of each other. Once launched, missiles would take approximately five minutes to reach their target. Given the short flight time, it is likely that military planners on both sides would plan to launch their missiles immediately upon receiving intelligence of an impending attack. In other words, if either nation believed itself to be under attack, it would probably respond instantly. The strategic intentions of policy-makers in both countries may well be entirely peaceable. But it is a simple and evident truth that if either country were not prepared to strike back, their warheads would not be weapons, but gilt-edged invitations for attack.

In moments of crisis, the intelligence services in both India and Pakistan are known to have extremely unreliable perceptions of threat. In a circumstance of heightened tension either country could well be provoked into launching a defensive attack based upon faulty intelligence. In an article published in the *New Yorker*, Seymour Hersh described an instance when such an attack had almost occurred in 1990. On that occasion Pakistani F-16s were spotted 'pre-positioned and armed for delivery'. Hersh quoted a U.S. government source as having said: '[This] was the most dangerous nuclear situation we have ever faced. . . . It may be as close as we've come to a nuclear exchange.'

The 1990 stand-off was provoked by events in Kashmir. India and Pakistan have already fought two wars over Kashmir. There is an enormous investment of public emotion on this issue in both countries.

Many of the Kashmir insurgents are battle-hardened veterans of the Afghan war. In recent months the conflict has spilled over from Kashmir into other parts of India, with civilian populations coming under attack in the neighbouring state of Himachal Pradesh. The Indian government has mooted the idea of launching 'hot pursuit' attacks across the Line of Control, against insurgents sheltering in Pakistan-held territory. In Pakistan such assaults are likely to be perceived as equivalent to an invasion. The risks of escalation are thus very real and are mounting every day.

Zia Miyan, a Pakistan-born nuclear expert at Princeton, said to me: 'There are soldiers on both sides who have a hankering for a grand act of heroic erasure. A day might well come when these people would say, "let's get it over with forever, once and for all, no matter what the cost." '

The geography of the subontinent is such as to ensure that the effects of a nuclear explosion on the northern plains would be felt across the entire region. The impact on Nepal for instance would be immediate.

In Kathmandu a magazine editor described to me how Nepali children celebrate the end of the monsoons and the shifting of the direction of the winds: they fly kites that sail eastwards. Through most of the year this is the direction of the prevalent winds, from west to east, from the Punjab plains, towards the mountains of Nepal. The jet stream blows hard and fast in this direction: the great plume that flutters like a pennant on the peak of Everest is actually a trail of windblown snow, blasted off the face of the mountain by the driving easterly wind. The winds change direction for only two or three months in the year, when the jet stream moves northwards. This is when the monsoons arrive, bringing sustenance to the parched landscapes of northern India, circling in a great sweep, westwards from the Bay of Bengal.

Kunda Dixit, a Kathmandu journalist and ecologist, explained to me that the monsoon months were the only time of year when it would be conceivable for India's military planners to launch a nuclear strike against Pakistan. At all other times 'it would be suicide'.

No matter what the direction of the winds or who the attacker, neither India nor Pakistan nor Nepal would escape the fallout. The mushroom clouds would shoot so high into the atmosphere that the effect of the earth's rotation would carry the radioactive plumes eastwards, over the high Himalayas and into the Tibetan plateau. 'In Nepal you would have radioactive snow', Kunda Dixit told me. 'The Tibetan plateau and the Himalayas are a water tower. Water is stored there as ice. In the hot season the snow melts and the rivers are full again. The reason Hindus regard mountains as being holy is because they give water — because of the natural processes by which, in the dry season, when there's no water anywhere else, the snow provides water. A lot of the names of our mountains are the

names of gods — Annapurna, means "giver of grain".
Of the rivers that flow out of Tibet, the Indus and
the Sutlej go westwards to the Arabian Sea. You
have the Brahmaputra flowing east. On the eastern
part of the Tibetan plateau you have the Irrawaddy,
the Salween, the Mekong and the Yangtze flowing
all the way to the Bay of Bengal and the South
China Sea. Tibet is sparsely populated but it is the
headwaters for half the world's population. The
snows of the Himalayas would become a vast reser-
voir of radioactivity.'

On a hot and humid August day, I drove around
New Delhi with an old friend, Kanti Bajpai,
trying to assess the damage the city would sustain in
the event of a nuclear explosion. Kanti has a doctorate in strategic studies from the University of
Illinois at Urbana-Champaign. His subject of research was India's nuclear programme. He has been
teaching at Jawaharlal Nehru University in New
Delhi since 1994. He is now an assistant professor
in disarmament studies.

Kanti was one among the many anti-nuclear
commentators and activists who went to work on
learning of the tests of 11 May. At that time, the
Bharatiya Janata Party's cadres were organizing
celebrations on the streets of several Indian cities.
Opposition politicians were left looking on in

stunned silence, struggling to gather their wits. It fell to citizens' associations, groups of activists and so on to take on the task of articulating a critical response to the tests. The well-known environmentalists Praful Bidwai and Achin Vinayak were two of the most prominent of these activists. Kanti came to national attention at this time, with his pointed critiques of the tests.

It so happens that Kanti is one of my oldest friends. We first met in school and have been close friends ever since. Kanti has changed the least of anyone I know: he is all joints and angles, thin and bespectacled. Even at the age of fifteen he had a slight, professorial stoop and an air of reflective abstraction.

After the tests, when I read Kanti's newspaper articles and watched him on television talk shows, defending his views with quiet tenacity, I thought back often to our three decades of discussion and disputation. I remembered how in school Kanti had always been fearless in defending unpopular positions. I was proud: time holds few satisfactions, I found, so pleasing as the validation of an early choice of friends.

Kanti has a reputation as a meticulous scholar and he pays careful attention to the arguments of the many strategists and defence experts who feel that India needs nuclear weapons. He is not dismissive of their positions, but he believes that on grounds of security, none of their arguments stand up to close scrutiny.

So far as Pakistan is concerned, Kanti believes that India, in pursuing a nuclear programme, has gambled away its single greatest military advantage: the overwhelming superiority of its conventional forces. In legitimizing Pakistan's nuclear programme India's military planners have, in effect, shot themselves in their feet. In relation to China, Kanti sees no realistic threat. He points out that there is no history of persistent antagonism between China and any region of the Indian subcontinent. No Chinese emperor has ever invaded India; no Indian has ever sought to conquer any part of China. Vietnam, Tibet, the Korean peninsula and Japan are areas which China's rulers have historically considered to be within their sphere of cultural and military influence. From these regions Chinese emperors regularly demanded tribute: it is with them that China has had recurrent problems in the twentieth century. This has never been the case with India. In thousands of years of close co-existence, Chinese and Indian soldiers have fought each other only once, during the war of 1962. This was a very brief conflict, fought on a sparsely-populated border. It had very little impact on the civilian populations of either country. In this war China fully attained its objectives which were to gain control of a strip of territory called Aksai Chin. China's leadership sees this area as a crucial strategic link between two of their provinces. There is absolutely no reason to believe that China has any further claims on India. Relations between the two countries were never better, Kanti points out, than just before the blasts of 11 May: this relationship now stands irreparably damaged.

Kanti is one of the many experts who believes that there is a real and pressing danger of nuclear war in the Indian subcontinent. Along with a number of other academic specialists he has been trying for some time to make an assessment of what the consequences of a nuclear war in South Asia would be. A friend of his, M.V. Ramanna, a research student in the Security Studies programme at MIT, had recently posted a draft of a research paper on the Internet. The paper was an analysis of the possible effects of a nuclear strike on Bombay. Ramanna had developed formulae for computing the effects of such an attack, in Indian conditions. The paper had caused much excitement in the community of the knowledgeable: it was more or less the first such study to be done of a South Asian city. Some of Ramanna's findings had caused surprise: the casualty rates that he cited, for instance, were lower than many had expected.

We set out on our journey of assessment armed with a copy of Ramanna's seminal paper. Kanti, like many other experts believes that the nuclear weapons that India and Pakistan currently possess are probably not greatly different, in destructive potential, from those that were dropped at Hiroshima and Nagasaki in 1947. It was on this assumption that Ramanna had based his calculations for Bombay. Kanti decided to follow his example.

We drove up Rajpath, the grand thoroughfare that separates North Block from South Block. Ahead lay the domed residence of the President, India's titular head of state and once the palace of the imperial British Viceroy: it is now known as Rashtrapati Bhavan. The palace looks down Rajpath, towards the ornamental India Gate. In the distance lie the ramparts of the Purana Qila, a sixteenth-century fort. This strip of land is the ceremonial centre of India: the place where the nation enacts many of its most solemn rituals of state.

Ground zero, Kanti said, would probably lie somewhere here: in all likelihood, in the exact centre of the roadway that separates North Block from South Block. The Prime Minister's office lies close at hand: so do those of the Foreign Minister and the Home Minister. The Defence Ministry office where I had visited George Fernandes is a little way away, on the far side of South Block.

On that occasion I'd asked Fernandes whether there were any shelters near by. No, he had told me, there were none, and nor were any being planned.

On detonation a nuclear weapon releases a burst of high-energy x-rays. These cause the temperature in the immediate vicinity of the point of explosion to rise very suddenly. According to Ramanna's calculations, the actual temperature would be well short of the theoretical limit of a hundred million degrees: it would reach only tens of millions of degrees.

The rise in temperature causes a fireball to form.

This fireball shoots outwards in every direction, cooling as it expands. By the time the fireball reached the facades of North Block and South Block it would probably have cooled to about 300,000 degrees. Although this would be no more than a fraction of its original temperature, it would be enough to kill every living thing within several hundred feet of the point of explosion. Those caught on open ground would evaporate: those shielded by the buildings' thick walls would be incinerated. The actual number of casualties would depend, of course, on the time of day and how many people were present in the area. The only certain casualties would be the troops of monkeys that reside permanently in the Blocks.

South Block and North Block, like many of the ceremonial buildings in New Delhi, are made principally of pink Rajasthan sandstone. In Hiroshima and Nagasaki granite surfaces and ceramic tiles were found to have melted up to several hundred feet from the points of explosion. Sandstone is considerably less dense than granite. The facades of the two Blocks would probably melt like candlewax; so would the dome and walls of Rashtrapati Bhavan and possibly even a portion of India Gate.

As it expands, the fireball generates twin shockwaves that eventually merge to form a single wave called the Mach front. This shockwave delivers a massive blow to everything in its path. This in turn is followed by an enormous increase in air pressure and very high wind velocities. The pressure of the air that follows in the wake of the Mach front can reach several thousand pounds per square inch: many thousand times greater than the pressure in the interior of a heated pressure cooker. This pressure in turn can generate winds that blow at speeds of more than two thousand miles per hour.

'Human beings will become projectiles', Kanti said. 'If you're in and around this area, and if you're not incinerated immediately you could be thrown at velocities of two hundred kilometres per hour yourself. You would become a bullet or a cannonshell.'

As we stood looking around us, at the great sunlit expanse of Rajpath, it struck me that the streets around us were lined with pointed lamp-posts and wrought iron fences. 'Objects on the ground will be tossed around at enormous velocity', Kanti said. 'The lamp-posts and fences would become missiles hurtling through the air.'

We drove away from the Blocks, towards the Yamuna river. On the way we passed the Parliament building: it is no more than a few hundred metres from the Blocks. Everyone here, Kanti said, would either be incinerated or killed by the radiation.

We drove past the National Archives, the Supreme Court and the vast bureaucratic warrens that house the government's principal tax offices. These too were within the radius of destruction where very little would survive apart from the external shells of the buildings. The whole recorded basis of government,

Kanti said, would vanish. Land records, taxation documents — almost everything that would be needed for the reconstruction of a settled society would perish within an instant of the blast.

We drove past the old Indian Express building, along the street where, on the election night of 1977, thousands had gathered to cheer the opposition's victory. I caught a glimpse of the newsroom where I'd held my first job. We were now at a distance of a couple of miles from ground zero.

The pressure caused by a nuclear explosion Kanti explained, even a relatively small one, was such that it sucked the air out of your body, so that your lungs burst. At a certain distance from the point of explosion you wouldn't necessarily die of burns or poisoning. 'If you were here your internal organs would rupture, even if you had survived the initial blasts and flying objects.'

Later, I asked Gautam Bhatia, a prominent Delhi architect, what the effects of the blast would be on the city's buildings. Weeks later he sent me a written assessment.

Many of the landmark buildings of British-era New Delhi, he writes, have very thick walls and are laterally buttressed with cross walls. This gives these buildings a honeycomb structure, making them very rigid and stable. They are capable of withstanding great pressure. But many of the city's well known contemporary buildings, like some of its five-star hotels, have glass curtain walls. In these, there would be: 'Instantaneous shattering, glass shards slicing through offices, people, furniture blown through the buildings. Not a happy sight. Such structures have a poor rating for withstanding pressure, poor facilities for egress and virtually no fire-fighting equipment.'

In the old part of the city, Bhatia writes, buildings are extremely flimsy. But these areas have one distinct advantage, which is that houses do not stand as individual structures in the landscape. 'They share party walls, like town houses, and internal rooms may at times be hidden away behind several layers of walls. This to some extent would help diffuse the lateral pressure of an explosion.'

The newer residential areas of New Delhi would fare very badly indeed. Most of the buildings in these areas are designed to withstand winds of about 160 kmph: in the event of a nuclear explosion they would face pressures of up to twenty times that. 'The walls would be blown away instantly; if columns and slabs remain, the pressure will rip the building out of its foundations and overturn it.'

Radiation from a nuclear explosion can set off fires for many miles. In Indian cities, many urban households use canisters of natural gas for everyday cooking. For miles around the point of explosions, Ramanna estimates, these canisters would burst into flames.

Ramanna, in his draft had estimated that in the event of a fifteen kiloton nuclear explosion in Bombay, the number of people who would die, over a period of a few weeks, would be somewhere between 150,000 to 800,000. Delhi is a city of about nine million, but its population is much more widely dispersed than that of Bombay. Kanti estimated that the casualty figures for Delhi would be much lower than those Ramanna had cited for Bombay: perhaps somewhere in the range of 200,000.

Kanti explained to me that the geographical spread of New Delhi is such that a single fifteen kiloton nuclear explosion could not destroy the whole conurbation. Only the central parts of the city would be directly affected by the blast. 'The city will continue to function in some way,' Kanti said, 'but its municipal, medical and police services will be in total chaos. The infrastructure will disappear.'

Later, in New York, I met Ramanna in person and asked for his own estimates for Delhi. The figures he cited were lower even than Kanti's: ranging from 60,000 to 180,000. He told me that in the event of similar explosions in the Pakistani cities of Karachi or Lahore, the figures for the former would be roughly similar to that of Bombay and of the latter to Delhi.

Fatalities however would account for only a small part of the human toll. Several hundreds of thousands of people will suffer burn injuries.

In Delhi, I met Dr Usha Srivastava, a member of a group called International Physicians for the Prevention of Nuclear War. She told me that over the last few decades, while Delhi's population had more than doubled, the total number of hospital beds in the city had increased only slightly. She estimated that there were only six to seven thousand beds in the government-run hospitals that cater to the majority of the city's population. These hospitals were already so crowded that in some wards three or four patients sometimes shared a single bed. The doctors in these hospitals routinely treated several dozen patients in the course of an hour.

New Delhi's major hospitals are all located within a few miles of the city's centre. They would not survive the blast. In all of India there is only one hospital ward that specializes in burn injuries. This is located in New Delhi and it can treat about two hundred patients at a time. This ward too would not survive.

In the event of a nuclear explosion in New Delhi, Dr Srivastava said softly: 'The ones who will be alive will be jealous of the dead ones.'

I began to wonder how the people of Delhi — or any other Indian or Pakistani city — would respond to a catastrophe of this kind. The question is not easily answered. India's civilian populations have on the whole been spared the conflicts and upheavals of the twentieth century. Neither of the World Wars touched the subcontinental mainland; in India there have been no revolutions and no military coups. The wars of the post-Independence era were fought by professional armies, in border areas, with very little collateral damage. Perhaps the most traumatic event in the history of modern India was the Partition of 1947. The singularity of the horror of this event was that in the main it involved civilian bloodshed: soldiers and modern weaponry were not involved in the slaughter.

Only one major Indian city has ever been bombed. This was Calcutta, in January 1942. A cluster of Japanese bombs fell on the centre of the city causing widespread panic. At about the same time, Rangoon, which was then a part of Britain's Indian Empire, was subjected to very heavy bombing by the Japanese. At the time Rangoon was populated largely by people from the Indian subcontinent — some sixty per cent of the citizenry is thought to have been of Indian descent.

This summer, in Calcutta, I interviewed several survivors of the Rangoon bombing. Many of them spoke of how, on the first day of the bombing — 24 December 1941 — they had run out into their gardens and into the streets to watch the Japanese planes coming in for their bombing runs. They had never imagined that war could come to their doorstep. They and their parents had disregarded warnings, paid no attention to signs of danger. They'd been absolutely confident that war would never intrude upon their lives: it hasn't happened before, why should it happen now?

When they finally recognized the enormity of what was under way, they left their houses and began to walk. Hundreds of thousands of people, mainly

Indians, took to the road, carrying a few belongings. The roads were soon too clogged to accommodate cars or buses: everyone had to walk, rich and poor, young and old. They walked all the way up the length of Burma and over the densely forested mountain ranges of eastern India. The British historian Hugh Tinker calls this 'The Forgotten Long March'. Some half a million people are thought to have taken to the road in this way: tens of thousands are thought to have died.

Something similar would happen, I suspect, in the aftermath of a nuclear explosion in either India or Pakistan. Millions and millions of people will begin to walk. Many will be nursing burn wounds and other severe injuries. There will be no food, no clean water and no prospect of medical care. Epidemics will break out.

I had always imagined that a nuclear blast was a kind of apocalypse, beyond which no existence could be contemplated. Like many Indians, the image that I had subconsciously associated with this eventuality was that of *pralay* — the mythological chaos of the end of the world. Listening to Kanti that day, as we drove around New Delhi, I realized that I, like most people, had been seduced into thinking of nuclear weapons in symbolic and mythic ways. The explosion that Kanti was describing would not constitute an apocalyptic ending: it would be a beginning. What would follow would make the prospect of an end an object of universal envy.

I think back often to the morning of 12 May. I was in New York then. I remember how amazed I was, not just at the news of India's nuclear tests, but also at the world's response: the tone of chastisement adopted by many Western countries, the finger-wagging by many who were themselves content to live under nuclear umbrellas. Had they imagined that nuclear technology had wound its way back into the genie's lamp simply because the Cold War had ended? Did they think that it had escaped the world's attention that between them the five peacekeepers of the United Nations' Security Council still possessed tens of thousands of nuclear warheads? If that were so, I remember thinking at the time, then perhaps India's nuclear tests had served a worthwhile purpose after all, by waking the world from this willed slumber.

So strong was my response against the implicit hypocrisy of the Western response that I discovered an unusual willingness in myself to put my own beliefs on nuclear matters aside. If there were good arguments to be made in defence of the Indian and Pakistani nuclear tests then I wanted to know what they were: I wanted to hear them for myself. What I heard instead was for the most part a strange mixture of psychologizing, grandiose fantasy and cynicism, allied with a deliberate conjuring up of illusory threats and imaginary fears.

The truth is that the motivation behind the Indian nuclear tests is simple. I once saw it summed up nicely: 'India's nuclear programme is status-driven, not threat driven.' In other words the primary intention behind the programme is to push India into an imagined circle of twice-born nations — 'the great powers'. India's nuclearists take it for granted that the blandness of their motivations will be sufficient to transform their nuclear weaponry into harmless symbols of status.

In Pakistan's case too the motivation behind the nuclear programme is similar: the status at issue here is parity with India. That the leaders of these two countries should be willing to run the risk of nuclear accidents, war, and economic breakdown in order to indulge these confused ambitions is itself a sign that some essential element in the social compact has broken down: that there is no longer any commensurability between the desires of the rulers and the well-being of the ruled.

There is a deepening crisis in India and Pakistan and the almost mystical hopes and beliefs that have come to be invested in nuclear technology are a symptom of this. The pursuit of nuclear weapons in the subcontinent is the moral equivalent of civil war: the targets the rulers have in mind for these weapons are, in the end, none other than their own people.

Acknowledgements

A shorter version of *Countdown* was published in 1998 by *The New Yorker*, by *Himal* magazine of Kathmandu, and by the *Ananda Bazar Patrika* of Calcutta, in Bengali translation. The government that was in power at the time of writing has since fallen. It was felt however that the material in *Countdown* was not so perishable as to have its fortunes tied to a moment of power: hence its publication in this form.

In the course of writing this piece I talked to many hundreds of people in India, Pakistan and Nepal. The impossiblity of severally listing these debts serves only to deepen my gratitude to those who took the time to meet me. This book would be incomplete, however, if I were not to acknowledge my gratitude to the following: Smt. Krishna Bose, M.P., Madiha Gauhar, Shahid Nadeem, Najam Sethi, Dr Durrsameem Ahmed, Eman Ahmed, Dr Zia Miyan, Dr M.V. Ramanna, Kunda Dixit, Kanak Dixit, Pritam and Meena Mansukhani, Radhika and Hari Sen, and my infinitely forbearing publisher Ravi Dayal. Dr Sunil Mukhi, Dr Sumit Ranjan Das, Dr Sourendu Gupta and other scientists at the Tata

Institute of Fundamental Research in Bombay were generous in giving of their time to discuss various aspects of the nuclear issue, from many different points of view: I owe them many thanks. I would also like to acknowledge the support of the *Ananda Bazaar Patrika*, *Himal* and *The New Yorker*. I am particularly indebted to Nandi Rodrigo, who did an astonishingly thorough job of fact checking my *New Yorker* piece, and to Bill Buford, who saw it to press. Madhumita Mazumdar contributed greatly to the background research and provided invaluable logistical support: I am deeply grateful to her.

Countdown owes its greatest debt to my wife, Deborah Baker. But for her urging I would never have committed myself to the many months of labour that went into the writing of this piece; nor would I be in a position to publish it today, in this form, if it were not for her editing. I owe her many, many thanks.